Believe, Live, Think:
TWO FEET IN

Heather Macy

with John Pennisi

This book contains information obtained from authentic and highly regarded sources. Reasonable efforts have been made to publish reliable data and information, but the author and publisher cannot assume responsibility for the validity of all materials or the consequences of their use.

ISBN: 978-0-9992125-9-2
Support@MHBookServices.com

Parts of this book are a work of fiction designed to help individuals understand how to be better teammates and more positive leaders. Names, characters, businesses, organizations, places, events, incidents, or locales are the product of the author's imagination or are used fictitiously. Any resemblance to actual persons, living or dead, or locales is entirely coincidental.

Cover Design & Illustrations: Callie Rector

FROM JOHN -

When Heather first approached me about writing this book, I was both excited and nervous.

She and I have been friends for over 20 years, but we'd never embarked on something as major as writing a book together. I'd been teaching English for 16 years when she approached me and had always dreamed of writing one, but I had no idea when or how that goal would come to fruition.

These last few months have been a whirlwind, to say the least. Writing a book has been one of the hardest – and most rewarding – experiences of my life.

I want to thank my parents and my sister, my teaching and coaching friends, my former (and current) players, and my former (and current) students. *And to my best friend, Patrick Behan (@BehanStrong), to whom this book is dedicated.* My life is an embarrassment of riches because of each and every one of you.

Today and Every Day, Believe in Miracles…

~ Heather

CONTENTS

INTRODUCTION

We – the team, the coaching staff, and I – believe that *Elite Performers Leave Nothing to Chance, Ever.*

Disciplined routines and habits are established to then call upon in both moments of great achievement and crushing adversity. In college athletics, we train to overcome all obstacles with grit and resiliency, and the level to which you prepare is critical for sustained success. The ability to adjust quickly becomes a needed skill in this quest for excellence.

We never anticipated having to train to depend on a coin toss.

However, we experienced that very scenario this past season.

We finished the regular season tied for first in our conference; our overall record was 25-1. Our only loss that season was a conference game on the road to the team we tied with for first. With our respective conference records of 17-1, we shared the regular season championship. The top seed in the tournament would be decided by the flip of a coin.

Yes, a coin flip.

I'm sure you can see where this is headed.

So, at 25-1 overall and tied for first in our conference, we found ourselves playing on the road in the semifinals of the conference tournament due to being on the unfortunate end of a coin flip.

We'd been consistent all year – *losing only one game and over the course of the season, having gone 70 days without a loss* – and yet we wouldn't host the semifinals or finals due to chance, something outside of our control, a scenario we simply could not have predicted.

So, there we were, on the road in the semifinals, the game being played on the #1 seed's campus. If we won, we'd probably see the host school again, but this time in the finals. We had beaten them at our place about a week prior, so the confidence was certainly there.

Then came the evening of February 25th. Game time. We were warming up like we normally do: disciplined and focused. We were getting a sweat going. I had a good feeling about the game in general. A good feeling about this team. This moment. This opportunity.

The basketball gods, however, had other ideas.

In a freak play, one of our most clutch players hit her head in the waning seconds of a very tight first half and was not cleared to play for the rest of the game. She was relegated to being a cheerleader behind our bench. The team was pressed, and we were not playing our best.

And our opponent? One of their guards ended up having the game of her life.

The second half wasn't close.

We lost by 14. To say we were in shock doesn't begin to describe the vibe.

And instead of immediately heading to the locker room to cry about our season having ended, however, the All-Conference awards were about to be handed out at mid-court. We were Co-Champions of the league that season, so we were going to be recognized. We had to stay on the court for a time, and it was tough. I simply wanted to be alone with the team in that moment.

When we finally returned to the locker room after the awards ceremony was over, we were obviously very upset. It's not every day you have the consistent type of success we'd had only to come up short when it matters most. We were all doing our best to manage our emotions and the reality of the moment.

But feelings aside, the logistics of when to return home came up.

We had planned on finishing the tournament as champions, so we'd made an itinerary that only went through the night of the first game. Losing had now messed things up, to say the least. *Should we still stay the night, or should we go home? We were only 3 hours away. We could be there by midnight.*

Something inside of me in that moment decided against doing that, the norm of how I'd treated each tournament over the last 21 years.

I found myself saying to the team, "We'll stay here and watch the next game."

We ate together as a team and then watched the host school win a close game that night. They would go on to win the conference championship on their home court the next day. They were going to the NCAA tournament.

Coin flip, remember?

So we watched the second semifinal game that night, and the team learned some really valuable lessons. We watched other players play, other coaches coach, other fans cheer. And watching something like that – all the while feeling that we were the ones who should have been out there – was a challenge, to say the least. But we weren't watching to scout a future opponent. We were taking the time to reflect on what had happened and making a collective vow for a different outcome next year.

Not one player was set to graduate, so God willing, everyone would be returning. We would take what we'd learned that night and grow.

After the game, we went back to the hotel. We would leave in the morning.

"Coach, what time?" the assistant coach asked me as we got to the hotel.

"Breakfast at 9. Get on the bus at 9:30," I say.

The next morning, I got up early – 6ish – had a healthy breakfast, worked out, read my devotional, read the Bible. And as I was sitting on the bed in my hotel room reading, my phone pinged with an incoming text message. It was 9:03 AM.

"Coach, everyone's down here for breakfast," my assistant said.

Because this was the first overnight trip we'd done all year – in *two* years, really – when I'd said, "Breakfast at 9," the team had assumed that everyone would eat together at that time. When I'd said it, however, I'd simply meant that everyone needed to eat around 9 at the latest, and then we'd get on the bus to head home.

But rather than tell my assistant to have everyone go on and eat, I thought God might be nudging me in a certain direction. So, I decided to take notice.

"I'll be right down," I said, acknowledging the "God wink" I was getting.

In the continental breakfast room of our hotel stood the entire team, packed up and ready to eat, luggage lined up against the wall. Many of them held the hotel receipt they'd had slipped under their doors that morning. This was all very new to them.

So, we ate as a team, and then I took the opportunity to get up and address the group while they were still hurt and stunned by the previous night's course of events. I'd had some time to think about previous seasons, about previous good-byes. The abruptness of the *business* of college sports. How things often turn on a dime.

I stood there that morning and talked to them about how two years prior when I was at a Junior College in South Carolina, we'd lost in the district championship game. This had been in March 2020. Everyone was then heading out on Spring Break, so amid the tears and disappointment at the end of our season, I'd said we'd meet up after Spring Break, talk about post-season work with the players (some of whom would be deciding on their 4-year college plan), summer plans, the whole nine yards. It was the standard end-of-season speech, to be honest. We didn't really say good-bye because we thought we'd see each other in a week. We'd had such a narrow focus on the season that I'd been completely unaware of early reports of coronavirus. Forgive me for not being more aware of what was going on in the world at that moment, but my "world" had been the team and our season. Everything else had been secondary. And honestly, that could have been said about the previous decade or so of my life: the vast majority of things had been secondary to my life as a college basketball coach.

Over Spring Break that year, I found myself at the ACC tournament in Greensboro. When the tournament itself was canceled, the virus finally had my attention, as it did much of the nation and world. And then the world as we know it changed, seemingly overnight.

So, while I initially thought I'd see the team again the week after Spring Break, I actually didn't see many of them in person again. Our sophomores finished the semester online. There was never a proper good-bye. There wasn't time for one.

I then talked to them about the time in October 2018 when I resigned from my head coaching position while in my 9th year as head coach. After the announcement that day, the team started pulling up to  the house to say goodbye. It was *rough*. It was abrupt. One of the hardest days of my life, to say the least. Their cars were all lined up in a single file down the street, parked, waiting to see me. I was on the phone with my agent, tears pouring down my face.

Yes, we were getting to say good-bye, but these were my girls. This was my family. It was more than good-bye. It was *loss*.

Again, things had turned on a dime.

So as I stood there that morning in the breakfast room of the hotel in Virginia, I told the team that yes, it was awful that we'd lost and that our season was over. But having lived through the pandemic and knowing how quickly things in life can and do change, there was still something to be said for us all being together that morning, eating, sharing a space, leaning on each other. There was something to be said for us *having a team*, being a part of something greater than ourselves as individuals.

There's something to be said for sticking together in a collective hurt and knowing that at the end of the day, things were going to get better. We had done so many cool things together, and we were not done.

And I'm convinced that because we'd stayed together following that loss – spent the night, eaten a couple of meals, shared a space – that we'd be all right. We were headed into the offseason, but I thought we'd be better than ever.

Offseasons in college sports can be tumultuous times. We currently find ourselves living in a world and in a basketball culture that constantly promotes the green grass on the other side of things.

"I didn't get playing time this year, so I'm out."

"Coach doesn't like me, so I'm out."

"This team doesn't get it – I'm their best player – and I'm only getting 15 minutes a game? I'm out."

And if we'd driven home the night of our semifinal loss, our players would have been isolated, many of them inundated with calls, texts, and everything else, including people chirping in their ear about this or that thing. This decision or that call.

That *could have* meant a major stop sign for our team.

But we hadn't done that. We'd stuck together that night, and the next morning, and on the bus ride home. I'd made a decision as the leader of this program to stay united amidst the adversity of that loss. Instead of selfishly wanting to head home and sleep in my own bed that night, I had put them first. I had chosen to be the servant leader I strive to be every single day of my life. I had made a choice, *a long-term choice.*

And instead of coming to a complete stop, I had chosen to lead the team in a way that *yielded and accelerated* us into the next phase of our basketball life: program development and growth. We weren't stopping. We weren't making knee-jerk reactions to anything that had happened. We would reflect on what happened, sure, but we would use all of it to strengthen our resolve as a unit.

And that's what this book is about: what it means to live a life with passion, consistency, and empathy. What it means to *yield* to life's hardships (stop signs) rather than exist in a stop-and-go mentality. How to know which exit to take – and how to avoid simply going in circles when you find yourself in one of life's *roundabouts.* How all this can impact your life, your mental health, and everyone around you.

And whether you're a basketball coach, a teacher, a nurse, a librarian, in IT, or a stay-at-home parent, *this book is for you.*

Adopting the strategies I write about in this book will (hopefully) help many of you live better, more fulfilling lives. And I'm hoping that these strategies help readers think about the roles and responsibilities they take on in their own lives, many of which often involve being a leader.

We all lead in different ways in our daily lives. Sometimes, we're successful. Many times, we're not. This book is for *everyone* in the sense that we're all met with daily decisions and choices to make, many of which affect other people. Many of which other people are *counting* on us to make, whether we want to make them or not.

Some people have embraced being a leader. Some feel as though it's been thrust upon them: undesirable but doable. And some want nothing to do with it.

I promise you: wherever you are in life, with whatever you're doing, and whomever you're doing it with...*this book is for you.*

I don't know everything there is to know about leadership, but I have learned a lot through failure and possess a willingness to share those lessons I've learned with others. There's not one way to lead, like there's no single best job out there, or no single best car out there.

As you join me for the journey we'll take together in this book, I'll talk about life's stop signs and its green lights. I'll talk about easing into and out of life's *roundabouts* – in other words, learning to yield and accelerate when you're in the roundabout – versus existing in a constant state of stop-and-go "traffic." I will share with you some stories from the road, *my* road. I know things now that I didn't know five years ago, ten years ago, and definitely some things I didn't know 20 years ago. We as human beings are constantly evolving, and that's partly the beauty of it. No matter what age you're at as you find yourself reading this book, you're not the same person you were a year ago. Five years ago. Ten years ago. And with that said, I hope this book helps you learn things about yourself – the current you, the one holding this book right now – including how to become the version of yourself you've always envisioned.

This book is for all of us.

Now let's do this, *TWO FEET IN* STYLE!

YOUR BODY
IS AN ENGINE

A year ago as I was brainstorming ideas for my next book, I was struck with the idea of using an automotive theme because so many words I live by – and lessons I've learned throughout the course of my life – relate to things we see and do on a daily basis as drivers: accelerate, hit the brakes, obey various signs, take an exit, and come to a stop. I'm constantly thinking and speaking in these terms, as well, not only with the team but also when I go to speaking engagements around the country. I believe it can be a very successful metaphor because it's relatable and there's some common ground there.

And whether you are the driver of a sports car, an SUV, a hybrid, or heck, even a tractor, the engine of that particular vehicle is an important part of the driving experience. That engine is what's going to get you from point to point safely and efficiently. While you may know nothing about engine types – a two-, four-, or six-cylinder, for example – it is vital that you really do examine that aspect of owning a car prior to signing on the dotted line, understanding that the engine relates to the concept of planning for your future.

For instance, if you're an outdoorsy person and you're literally attempting to get to the top of a mountain, a two-cylinder engine might not get you there.

If you're planning on living a quiet life of retirement in the suburbs, you probably won't need a six-cylinder.

These things matter.

The *insides* of the car matter, more so than you may initially think.

I know a lot of people who do virtually no research about car-buying before going to the lot, and they simply make a gut decision when they get there. Now, it's hard to argue against the power of a gut feeling – we've all been there. However, if you've only got one shot to get it right, you might want to spend some time thinking about it. In other words, if you only had one shot to pick a partner in life…wouldn't you want to take your time to get it right?

That leads me to one of the many mantras I have come to live by:

Whatever's inside is going to come out.

It's essentially a metaphor about the things we put into our bodies. And when I say *things*, I'm talking about anything and everything: food, drink, love, healthy and unhealthy habits, anger, secrets, lies, etc. If it's inside you, I promise you: one day, it will come out!

Before we dive into this concept, I'm not saying this to scare you. I'm saying this because it's something that took me a while to learn, and one key purpose of this book is to pass on the things I wished I'd learned much earlier on in my life.

Let's look at an example of behavior that illustrates this concept. Sometimes when I see a coach yell at his or her team or go off on an official, I think about how much hurt that person must be experiencing in order to be so reactive. I'm not passing judgment because I've certainly lost my cool on the sideline at various moments of my career, but I've also learned from those moments. I use this example of coaching behavior to show that when people hurt that badly on the inside, that hurt is going to manifest itself somehow. It has to! You can only bottle those things up for so long. And often when it does, it's not pretty, and there can be some major consequences.

So all this is to say that as a person navigating your life and *as a leader* – whether you're a Division 1 head basketball coach, a stay-at-home parent, a pediatrician, or a classroom teacher – you have to positively fuel yourself in order to achieve what you want to achieve, right? You have to put *fuel* into your body – literally and metaphorically – that will take you to the next level. Fuel that will lead you to that next goal, that next dream.

The good news is that there are lots of things that qualify as fuel, and finding a balance among them all is key.

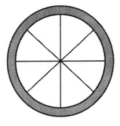

Food might be number one on the list. Nutrients. The *literal* fuel you need to carry out your day and lead a healthy life.

Hydration is fuel.

Sleep is fuel.

Exercise and **movement** are fuel.

Recovery is also fuel.

If you're lucky, **family** can be your fuel. Time spent with loved ones.

Faith in God and/or **spirituality** can also be fuel, maybe the most important fuel in the long run.

These are all things you put into your body in order to move yourself along in life. And if you're in a spot where you can maintain a balance among a variety of fuel *sources*, you'll probably be feeling pretty good about things. And you should! Balance is key in so many things in life.

However, if you're fueling your body in an imbalanced way – overeating, partaking in substance abuse, not getting enough sleep, having little to no down time – then it will be impossible for you to move about life the way you really want. Your body's *engine* will be dead on arrival.

And what's inside is eventually going to come out.

Food

To be completely honest, there have been times in my life when I would eat as a coping mechanism for stress. When we find ourselves in stressful situations or situations in which we feel we have little to no control, many of us find solace in food.

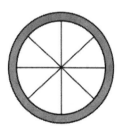

I remember times when I would come into the office in the morning, and the only way I could get through the morning would be by eating an entire bag of gummy bears.

That was my fuel, and it was purely transactional. *Eat this bag of candy? Get through the morning.* On some days, I would also forego lunch entirely, for example. Not only is this type of living unsustainable, but it's completely unhealthy, right? However, when many of us let stress run our lives, we also let it *ruin* our lives. And food is a quick way to ruin your life.

I was gaining weight and feeling awful about myself. But logically, I was fueling my body with garbage, so those feelings of inadequacy and insecurity made sense! And also, because I was putting bad things into my body, bad things would often come out!

I'd be angry, moody, irritable.

I'd snap at friends, co-workers, and family.

Not good, right?

I could wax poetic on the importance of nutrition and a balanced diet for an entire book. Suffice it to say, if you're fueling your body with a balanced diet and a variety of the other types of healthy *fuel*, you're setting yourself up for success in everything you do.

Hydration

When I was at that time in my life when stress ruled my day, I used to think, *If one more person tells me to stay hydrated, I'm going to scream!*

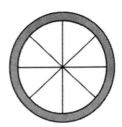

But they were often right!

The fact that this is such a relatively easy thing to manage and yet gets overlooked by so many people is mind-boggling. We are blessed to live in a country where the vast majority of us have access to clean, drinkable water. Yet millions of Americans are habitually dehydrated. As I'm writing this sentence, I'm reminding myself that I haven't had enough water today, so I can be guilty of this too. But our bodies are roughly 60% water, right? So water is quite literally a major source of fuel that can support healthy living and us feeling good about ourselves.

It may sound so simple, but drinking lots of water each day will keep your mind and body on the right path. You'll need to acquire the habit in the first place, so start small and build from there. I stay motivated to drink more water by making this simple promise: every time a negative thought or doubt creeps into my mind, I drink three big gulps of water. This does help me stay hydrated, obviously. However, it also helps me view negative thoughts and doubts as things that simply *flow through me*, and water helps with that flow.

Lastly, drinking more water will inherently make you feel less of a need for other liquids: coffee, soda, and alcohol. It's a win-win.

Sleep

Who out there doesn't love getting a good night's sleep?

I don't know a single person who wakes up after a night of tossing and turning and says, *That felt great!*

I know that everybody's body is different, but we as human beings all

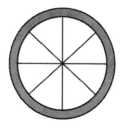

benefit from getting quality sleep. Whether your body needs a full 8-9 hours or only 5-6 hours to fully function the next day, sleep matters. It's essentially brain recovery! Studies show that sound sleep recharges our bodies, helps us process knowledge and memory, boosts our immune system, and increases productivity (among other benefits). Sleep is the "compound interest" of the body: it does the work while we are unconscious in our beds.

I also wanted to pass along something that goes against what many of us have heard about rest, sleep, and routines.

I know without the shadow of a doubt that many of us have heard about the importance of a morning routine. How the 1% get up in the morning and attack their day!

Truthfully, I like to think in terms of the 3%. The 3% are those elite performers who are motivated from within to push themselves to achieve excellence and put in the work, while the other 97% are wasting the day that God has granted them. To me, success is about habits, and I strive to acquire and maintain habits of the 3%. I'm not interested in letting my day slip by, a day that's been given to me *as a gift*. I'm interested in maximizing each day but doing so in a responsible way that allows me to take care of my mind, body, and soul.

I want to be clear: I think *Rise and Grind* culture can be very damaging because it often ignores the need for sleep, down time, and self-care. What I want to encourage you to do – and what I do in my own life – is work hard each day in a way that pushes you to do your best and excel while also taking care of yourself and those around you.

So with regard to sleep specifically, the 3% includes those people who are not only getting up early to do that morning routine, but they're also winding down in the evening with a beneficial and balanced *night* routine. The next chapter in the book is dedicated entirely to the concept of yielding because I believe it's so important. In brief, I encourage you to have a morning routine that allows you time to yield into your day as I would encourage you to have a similar routine in the evening: a period of time in which you *yield into* falling asleep and (hopefully) thereby get good, *quality* sleep.

And no, the concept of a nightly routine does not mean subscribing to the notion of "It's Wine O'clock Somewhere" or binging the latest Netflix series that's all the rage. Those things are really, at their core, coping mechanisms more than anything else. And we're not shooting for coping mechanisms as elite performers and leaders. We're shooting for quality time that's purposeful and intentional, time that allows your brain to recover while you process your day and prepare for the next one.

My nightly routine, for example, involves any or all of the following: lighting a candle, taking a bath, reading a book, writing in my journal, drinking plenty of water, and going to sleep early. Notice that none of that involves a screen.

And I give myself hours to do those things. *Hours.*

Feel free to also use my rule that nothing with 5G should ever find its way into your bedroom!

It's true, though. How many of us have spent hours at night doom-scrolling through Instagram or other social media? That's not a good nightly routine. It's the opposite of one, in fact. Think about how that type of behavior impacts romantic relationships, as well. Nighttime should be a special time for both you and your partner. How attractive do you think you're going to look when you're in bed on your phone for the umpteenth time? Also, isolating oneself can be the gateway drug for other bad habits to emerge.

I would really encourage everyone to reflect on both their morning and night routines (especially if you don't currently have one). How we begin and end our day is so important.

Movement and Exercise

As I said, a good night's sleep will leave you feeling better and will help you be more productive, especially when it comes to movement and exercise. While we live in a world that has produced a big box gym culture that may be too much for some to handle, exercising is vital to our long-term health. And it 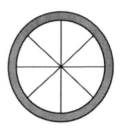 shouldn't take signing up for a boot camp with 30 other people or a cycling class with someone screaming in your face to motivate you.

I've always said that *fitness is a relationship between you and you*. It's personal. Make it about you and push yourself to stay active, even on days when you convince yourself to stay on the couch or ignore your after-dinner walk.

The great thing about exercising is that any movement is better than no movement. Whether it's a 5-mile run to start your day or a session of hot yoga after a long day at work, you're doing your body a favor. Also, partaking in a regular exercise routine will help you sleep better in the long run.

I've always believed that *consistency is the truest measure of performance*. This especially true when it comes to exercise and nutrition. You didn't gain 30 pounds with one cheeseburger, nor did you get in shape with a single bike ride. It's about a consistent commitment to eating healthy and *moving*. It's true that often, the most difficult step can often be the first one: putting on those running shoes and getting out the door, pressing play on that cardio video on YouTube, or signing up for that exercise class at your local gym. But I would encourage you to *keep showing up* once you get over your initial reluctance. Society often tells us to quit, but you will find success if you *keep showing up*.

Also, please forgive yourself if you have a moment of indulgence or forget about *clean eating* for one meal. I had a college roommate who taught me that you can "mess up" every now and again but still be on the straight and narrow to your ultimate goal. One bad meal isn't the end of the world, but don't let one bad meal turn into a week of bad meals. Recognize a mistake for what it is – a mistake – and then adjust and move forward.

Speaking of moving forward: motion is the lotion. Being active is going to pay dividends in so many ways. So go out there and get moving!

Recovery

Full disclosure: we live in a world that often views down time as laziness, pure and simple. Recovery and down time are simply counter cultural to the world of *go go go*.

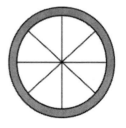

Many people think that if you're on the couch reading a book or, heaven forbid, taking a nap in the afternoon, you're not being productive! *You're being a sad sack! Get up and do something with your life, why dontcha?!*

The truth is, recovery is as important as the workout. People often forget that. For example, people who work out habitually also know that they *have* to take days off from time to time. If you work out literally every day, your body will shift at some point into being in crisis mode around the clock. There must be days in which you rest and recover from your workout routine. The body needs time to heal. When the body heals, the heart also heals; we often forget about attending to our social emotional wounds as adults, but it's got to be part of the conversation. Recovery can help with that.

Also, recovery is important for everyone, even those who don't routinely work out in the conventional sense. I'm assuming that many people reading this book have a job of some sort. Maybe it's a job in which you earn a paycheck, or it could be the job of being a parent. Regardless of the job title itself, you know there are moments when you have to be *on* (your working hours). When we're *on*, we're often running on the adrenaline of the moment. In my own experience, for example, it's hard to be *tired* when I'm coaching a college basketball game.

If you don't work in some down time and recovery, however, the moment you are no longer "on" may bring you to the fetal position. This also relates to what I call *yielding* in and out of life's experiences: moving between parts of our lives in a way that makes sense, a way that fosters growth and self-care.

In other words, did you spend enough time at home in the morning taking care of *yourself* before going to work? Did you lay some "green bricks" to start your day off on the right foot? A green brick is anything you do to build a foundation for clarity and having a sound mind, body, and spirit. Specifically, green bricks in the morning can be time for meditation, a healthy breakfast, reading the Bible or a daily devotional, or simply sitting in silence for a time.

So, did you get up 90 minutes before you had to leave the house and focus on the 3 G's: God, Gratitude, and Green Bricks? Or did you wake up 20 minutes before you had to get out the door, and those 20 short minutes included a shower, getting dressed, your hygiene routine, and breakfast?

Guess who's probably going to have a better day at work? (Hint: it's not the person who was awake and out the door in a feverish 20 minutes!)

My point is this: recovery is as important as the other parts of one's day, but it's also a part of life that is often looked down on or completely ignored.

Recovery is important. Remember that.

Family

If you're blessed with a loving family as am I, you already know how important this type of *fuel* is. My family knows me better than anyone else, and they have been a constant support to me for my entire life. My parents especially. Having 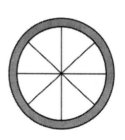 them watch me from the stands as a player at Greensboro College to having them watch me from the stands as the head coach of that very same basketball program has been truly special.

However, I know that not everyone's life is like mine.

Some people come from a broken home, have experienced the death of a parent or sibling, have dealt with a family member's addiction, or simply don't have a relationship with their existing family members. We're all different, so this type of *fuel* – spending time with one's blood relatives – can be tricky for many people. And I get it.

If family is not a source of fuel for you, then that's perfectly okay. But I want to make something clear, as well.

Family doesn't have to mean only blood relatives. For many of us, we have chosen a family of friends to help us move through life. People we're not related to, but who have become so close to us over the years.

For example, my co-author of this book, John Pennisi, and I have known each other for 20 years. We met at Lenoir-Rhyne College (now University) in the fall of 2001 when I was a first-year assistant coach and he was a freshman manager for our women's basketball team. He and I have been through it, let me tell you! You see, that one year we were at LR together, we learned some valuable lessons about life and relationships and forgiveness that, we believe, laid the groundwork for our lasting friendship.

At the time, I was 23, in my second year of college coaching, and still at that point in my career when there was no limit on how many hours I would spend in the office on any given day. I was always looking for more things to do, and it's safe to say that I did not have a healthy balance between my work life and my personal life.

That same year, John was 18 and in his freshman year of college. He had his own academic and social priorities to manage, and then only two weeks into the school year, the tragic events of September 11th occurred. For someone who'd lived his entire life several states away, being away from home at such a tumultuous time in our country's history was difficult for him, to say the least. After the first two games of our season toward the end of November, he had to step away from our team to get some things in order.

At the time, I was very upset with him. In the months he'd been with our program, he had become a vital part of our team and its chemistry. He was upset too, having to take time away, but felt strongly that it was something he had to do.

To be honest, we didn't speak for some time.

Our season kept going, obviously, and he had exams and then went home for the holidays. When he returned to Hickory that January, the head coach of the team and I asked him to come back as manager. We would help him manage the responsibilities that he had with the team while supporting his work in the classroom. He would help us out by resuming many of his former duties and help us finish out the season. Thankfully, he decided to return to the team, and we ended up having a successful season.

I tell this story to offer up a time when two people had to "die" to their own ego in order to remedy a situation. (Dying to your own ego is such an important concept that I've dedicated all of Chapter 6 to it.) If one of us hadn't been willing to put the other person's needs ahead of our own, who knows what would have happened? Instead, we've been friends for 20 years, and that's a beautiful thing.

I want to encourage all of you to be open to new friendships, as many of us know that friendship can be such a sustenance. Friends can be there for you in ways that family members often simply cannot be. And that's not their fault; it's simply that certain friendships can be a way for us to recharge and fuel our bodies and minds.

Real friends also tell you the truth.

John and I both saw that play out during our year together at LR, and I've come back to this idea many times over the years. Sometimes, a friend has to tell you what you want to hear, but ultimately, that same person will tell you what you *need* to hear when it matters most. And often, hearing the truth from someone we're not related to by blood can be very impactful. I know John's told me the truth over the years, as I have with him. And we thank each other every day for that.

Find friends who will tell you the truth!

Faith and Spirituality

I've saved this one for last even though for many, it's the most important aspect of one's life, myself included.

Personally speaking, my faith is the rock upon which I live my life. There has been no more grounding 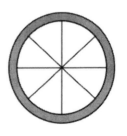 influence in my life than my faith in and relationship with God. I'm someone who grew up in the church, and as a child and adolescent, I understood things about God and the Bible and how I was supposed to live my life according to His way. But now as an adult, I have a *relationship* with Him. It's not only about going to church and listening to scripture – *going through the motions* – like I often did as a child. Now, I make the conscious daily effort to work on my relationship with Him. Regardless of the day or week I've had – lost a game, argued with a friend, got upset over something trivial – it all falls away when I focus on my relationship with God. I talk to Him. When I feel broken, I pray to Him. I give it all up to Him: both the blessings and the challenges.

It's safe to say that I am not quite sure where I'd be today without having built a relationship with God.

And let me be the first to say that I don't think I have a perfect one. Far from it. But it's a relationship that I'm constantly working on and learning from and growing toward. When I start to lose myself in negative thoughts, I lean back into His love and grace.

Lastly, whether you are a follower of a specific religion or you simply possess a certain spirituality, this can be a source of great strength and fuel in one's life. It can be the *multiplier* that enhances every other aspect of your life exponentially.

So, whether you're someone who routinely gets a good night's sleep and eats a healthy diet or someone who wants to improve in any or all of the above facets of life, I hope you can acknowledge how important your body's fuel is to both your mindset and your physical well-being. What we put into our bodies matters. And while I'm not perfect, I'm perfectly imperfect. I know this about myself and am working on improving every single day. I want this life-changing experience to happen for you too!

LEARNING TO YIELD & ACCELERATE

So now that we've talked about the body being an engine that makes us *go*, let's move on to that feeling many of us have had when we finally got behind the wheel of a car. For many of us, it was when we were 15 or 16 and were first learning to drive. Maybe it was the day you got your permit and finally took the family minivan for a spin (parent in tow), or maybe it's simply the feeling of driving with the windows down, favorite song on the radio, and not a care in the world.

I'm aware that not everyone out there is able to drive or has ever driven a car, but I'm willing to bet that everyone reading this book has had to depend on some sort of transportation at some point in your life. I hope that everyone reading this book can relate to driving in some way, whether you've done it yourself or have been a passenger in a vehicle outside of your control. It all counts!

With that said, once you find yourself behind the wheel of a car (or are a passenger in one), that experience can be both exhilarating and scary. Exhilarating because of the concept of the journey: you're headed from one place to the next, and there can be a lot of excitement about getting to that destination. Scary because there are a lot of unknowns when it comes to travel. How long will it take to get there? How much will it cost? How safe is it? Will I meet anyone interesting along the way?

There's also inherently a lot of *anticipation* when it comes to driving and the idea of staring out at the horizon, heading toward that destination. When we head to that destination, we know what we want, in a way. We can see it lying ahead, and we want to get there.

We get in the car to have it take us somewhere, right? And hopefully in life, you're getting to choose that destination.

So, let's talk about these concepts of choice and desire.

I think we've all had those moments in life when we think we know what we want: we see something in front of us, whether it be material (the latest iPhone) or more abstract (finally picking up the paintbrush and becoming the artist we've always dreamed of becoming), and we take it! In doing so, we often ignore others' opinions around us. We know what's best for ourselves, right? So, everyone else needs to get out of the way and let us do our thing.

But too often in life do we pursue things that are simply fleeting or temporary. Even when we set an important goal for ourselves, one of two things often happens:

1. We achieve the goal and then start immediately clamoring for the next best thing or a different, loftier goal.

2. We fall short of the goal or fail completely and then begin a downward spiral in which our self-worth takes a major hit.

We also often anticipate the wrong thing or think our future self will want this thing or that achievement when in fact, that couldn't be further from the truth.

In other words, we're often planning for the right reasons, but our focus is often on the wrong stuff.

Imagine a race car driver whose goal is to win the Indianapolis 500. Great goal, right? Absolutely. And it's one that requires countless hours of preparation.

This person spends weeks, months, and even years preparing for this goal.

And the goal is to win, right?

Great.

But what happens if this driver comes in 2nd? Or what if the driver comes in 10th? Or what if the driver doesn't even finish the race because they blow a tire and crash into the wall? Those are all distinct possibilities, right?

If the driver doesn't come in first, then they're left thinking about everything they did to prepare for the race...all the hours behind the wheel, the time spent with the team, anticipating problems during the race itself. The driver did it all. And in doing so, they feel that they did the best they could've done.

But it wasn't enough. And in life, it often *isn't* enough.

This moment is what I call one of life's stop signs.

Those moments of crushing defeat that life is bound to hand us from time to time. It's not about whether or not we will encounter moments like these in our own lifetimes.

We will.

It's really about what happens *next*.

The driver in this scenario has spent all this time preparing for that single goal and ultimately failed. They quite literally lost the race. And along the way, either consciously or subconsciously, they came to define their entire existence on *winning* that race. With this failure...there's a lot of confusion and hurt and despair. And rightfully so.

So where do they go from here? What do they do *now*?

Let's talk about it.

Yielding vs. a Life of Stop-and-Go

Failing at something we put a lot of time, effort, and energy into can be devastating.

Depending on the magnitude and scope of the failure itself, it can cause us to spend three days on the couch eating ice cream or send us into a full-blown mental breakdown. Maybe some of you reading this right now have experienced something along this spectrum.

I think that this devastation we sometimes feel, this feeling that we're not good enough and will never achieve our true goals and aspirations, pertains to this state of being that many of us – my past self included – subscribe to: living a life in terms of stop signs.

What do I mean by this exactly?

It means that our lives are *go go go* until we meet a goal we've set for ourselves, and then boom! The goal's been met (or we failed to meet it), and now we don't know what to do with ourselves.

The race car driver loses the race and picks up drinking to cope with the loss.

A high school senior doesn't get into her dream school and reconsiders whether she even wants to go to college at all.

A man spends years looking forward to retirement, only to be immediately bored and lonely with his newfound lifestyle.

Sometimes, people spend so much time *When/Then* thinking ("*When* I retire, *then* I'll travel the world."), that they often end up never doing what they set out to do! I hate to say it, but retirement can be difficult for many people, especially the ones who've spent their whole lives working incredibly hard to achieve this as their *destination goal*. Retirement is the stop sign, and once they get there, they have no idea what to do next. It's awful, but you often hear of people hitting the retirement age and then dying soon thereafter because they can't manage to yield from a high-intensity work life to the much slower pace of retirement.

And as a basketball coach, the season is very much *go go go* until it isn't, right? That last loss of every season is the stop sign, if you're not careful. And my past self would often crash and spend days on end afterward feeling unmoored and purposeless. So much would ride on every season that if we didn't end up winning a championship – regular season or postseason – the season would end with a loss, and the whole thing felt like one giant failure. Because the fact of the matter is this: there's only one winner at the end of a sports season. And if that winner isn't you and your team, that feeling of failure can stay with you indefinitely if you're not careful. You can stay stuck in a roundabout, unable to make the next choice, or take the correct "exit" to get to the next stage of your life.

You know that single lane on the inside of every roundabout you come across on the road? The one that you could stay in and theoretically go around and around in forever? Some people stay stuck in that lane in their own lives, afraid or unwilling to make the hard choice about what comes next. Many of these people live their lives in terms of stop signs – setting singular goals that result in confusion or ambivalence. They're not used to what comes next when we find ourselves in one of life's roundabouts and then have to make some powerful choices. They *sit this one out*, as they say.

This all leads me to say that over the years, instead of living in terms of stop signs, I have trained myself to *yield* in and out of life's roundabouts, moments and times that include the day-to-day all the way to major life events. Often, it's easy for me to view my own life in terms of roundabouts because my life has a very clean delineation between *season* and *offseason*. But a roundabout could be any period of time or significant moment, one that you know will come to an end or one that has no end in sight. These roundabouts can be periods of positivity, loss, celebration, or anticipation. They can involve a variety of emotions. Viewing life in terms of roundabouts – instead of stop signs – is vital to living a balanced and ordered life. It allows you to acknowledge that significant things are going to happen to you in your life – both good and bad – and that regardless of the *thing* itself, you have a way of managing your world and your emotions as you yield and then accelerate into the next phase of your life. It's not about planning for a certain outcome. It's about having a holistic perspective on life that allows you to prepare for change and what that brings.

Viewing my life in terms of roundabouts and staying centered throughout my day-to-day life – weathering life's highs and the lows by yielding and refusing to let my emotions dictate my life – has added years to my life. I'm sure of it.

So, you may be asking yourself, how does any of this apply to *me*? Let's talk about it.

I think there's a feeling we've all had at some point in our lives, to some degree.

We've worked really hard for something, and then we may get complacent, or a bit full of ourselves, or lose sight of the prize. Keeping up with the Joneses is a real thing, and it's something we've all seen or even done ourselves. This idea of projecting success or wanting others to perceive us as being successful.

So instead of placing value in a tangible *thing* or in a *result*, I would argue that the journey is the prize.

You heard me.

The *journey*.

So often in life do we look ahead at a goal or a reward as an endline and think: *This is it. Once I'm there, I'm there. It's over. I will have accomplished all I need to accomplish.*

For many people in college sports, for example, this goal is often a championship. Whether it's a regular season championship, a conference tournament championship, or a national championship. It's true: many college teams out there set a goal of winning a national championship – that's well within their right, and in some cases, it's also the expectation of their boosters, fan base, and their entire university – but that goal in and of itself is a sham.

It is a sham because you have to love the things in life (*the people*) that love you back.

If you're working around the clock for a goal such as that, you are setting yourself up for failure. If that's the only thing that gets you out of bed in the morning, watch out. That's what I've been referring to as this concept of yielding in and out of life's seasons. The people who define their entire existence around that singular end goal – one with a finite end result – are the ones who often fail, no matter what.

Even if they achieve that goal, for many of them there's a momentary celebration, and then it's on to the next one.

I worked with a coach at one point in my life who had an odd way of looking at wins.

"Whew, at least we didn't lose," she'd say, semi-seriously.

Huh?

At least we didn't lose?! What the heck kind of philosophy is that? I know now that it's a philosophy *based in fear*.

But that's the way some coaches – and some people – live. There's a sigh of relief when they win – no real celebration – but then all heck breaks loose with a loss.

That's gotta be awful, right?

So let me get back to the concept of yielding.

In a yielding mindset, you *understand* that change in life is inevitable. It's going to happen whether you like it or not. What's that old adage? Human beings make plans, and God laughs. He's laughing because we can make all the plans we want, but ultimately, He's the one in charge, right? So let's change the wording a bit.

Instead of making plans, we *prepare*. And part of preparing for what comes next – especially in a world that is routinely unpredictable – includes yielding.

When we learn to yield in life, we understand that things are going to change. Plans are going to get broken. Even the most solid of plans oftentimes fail. It's not a matter of if. It's a matter of when. And the "when" could strike at any moment. So when we're learning to yield, we understand that change could happen at any moment, *and that's okay*.

It's okay.

Change is okay.

Stagnation is equal to death, as far as I'm concerned.

Statis (being *static*) is the absence of movement, right? The absence of change.

Who's interested in being static? Certainly not me.

We've gotta keep this thing going, right?

Life is going to keep going, whether we like it or not. So don't we need to learn how to adapt and change in order to survive? Absolutely.

This is where yielding is key. With yielding, you know you're going to experience changes in your life, and you're okay with it. You're preparing for it. You're thinking ahead. You're *anticipating*.

And so the goal is never one thing.

It's never one thing.

It's never about winning a single championship. It's about building a winning *program*.

It's never about earning a single promotion. It's about making a *career* for yourself that you can be proud of for the next 30 years.

In marriage, it's never about the wedding itself. It's about loving your soulmate the way he or she deserves to be loved, today and every day.

The journey is the prize, and we've got to have faith and *accelerate* out of the roundabout to get there.

Let me be clear about something while we're on this topic. Of course, it's important to set goals in life; I would never tell you not to. And the *wording* and *timing* of your goals matter. For example, saying, "I want to *get* married," versus saying, "I want to be *happily* married." There's a difference there, for sure.

Yes, goal setting is important; however, once those goals are set, you need to be engaged and enjoy the ride. *The ride* is where the best stories happen.

For instance, some of my best memories from my coaching career are from practices. They're from team bonding activities outside the gym. They're from community service projects we did. They're from bus rides to and from games.

Sure, wins are wonderful. Championships? Even better.

But as someone who's won over 300 games, I can tell you that the number doesn't amount to a hill of beans without the people who helped you get there. I couldn't have won a single game without the young ladies who played for me, the assistant coaches who worked with me, and the athletic directors and chancellors who hired me. They have all been a part of my journey, and I've enjoyed every bit of it.

So, let me give you a scenario.

Say we meet a head coach whose utmost goal for her season is to win a national championship. She feels strongly that she's got the young ladies on her team who can win it, the staff who can help everyone get there, and the fan base who can cheer them all on. And she works from dawn til dusk to make it happen. She's singularly focused on that one goal, letting her personal relationships suffer the entire time. She's got no time for anything or anyone else.

And as she and her team move through that season, she's losing her mind over each loss and having a sigh of relief when they win. She's praying that their backup point guard will come back sooner than later from her injury, and that the team chemistry will improve in time for the postseason.

But then, two weeks before the conference tournament, her best player – a small forward who leads the conference in scoring and rebounding – tears her ACL.

Everyone's devastated, to say the least. That's a tough injury to rehab from, as many of us know, and to make matters worse, the player was a 5th-year senior. She's done. There are tears from everyone, head coach included.

The team goes on to lose in the conference tournament finals, and they do not get an at-large bid to the NCAA tournament. Their season is over.

Now, without seeing this play out in real life, can't we still imagine how that head coach will feel after that final loss? It's not going to be pretty, to say the least.

She's bet her entire season on a national championship – a lofty goal, even for the most prestigious women's basketball programs in the country – and she's come up short.

To her, nothing matters because the team did not achieve the goal. They didn't even come close, in actuality.

That can't be a healthy way to live, right? There's no way.

However, if that coach had learned to yield in and out of life's *seasons*, she could have prepared for that national championship knowing full well that the end goal is not the only thing that matters. And that win, lose, or draw, life would continue after that final game, regardless of the end result.

Yielding prevents these types of breakdowns because it reinforces a lifelong purpose.

It reinforces the idea that your worth as a person is not based on a single goal, a single trifle in the grand scheme of all things in the universe. You set goals, sure – healthy ones – and you can give those goals your all while simultaneously knowing that meeting or not meeting the goals is not a direct reflection of your DNA.

Losing in the conference finals doesn't make you a bad coach, or a bad person.

Winning that same game doesn't mean you're a *good* person.

However, being hyper-focused and ignoring the journey itself – that's a recipe for disaster.

Because remember that head coach we were talking about a few pages ago? She's downright miserable after that last game. She's fallen short of the goal and is broken. She's isolated herself in a big way, and she's lonely. She's been stuck in a roundabout, going in the wrong direction for months and months.

And the unfortunate thing is that she's missed all the good stuff along the way.

She's missed all the team bonding activities in the preseason because all she could think about was their first opponent on the schedule.

She's missed all the fun on the bus for away games because she was too busy reviewing game plans and watching film.

She's let her relationships suffer with family and friends.

She's missed the joys of practice, those moments when the team truly gets better. When individual players get better.

There's a joy to being a coach, and being solely focused on your win-loss record or how many championships you win is setting yourself up to always be disappointed, to always miss those moments with your players and staff that mean the most.

As I mentioned before, yes, I've won 300 games. However, I've won far fewer championships in my years as a coach. Therefore, if I only defined success by championships, I'd be sorely disappointed after a 20+ year coaching career. If that were my only goal, I would have missed out on so much.

And so this is one of the most major topics I want to touch upon in this book: learning to yield in and out of life's seasons. Weathering the storm that you know full well is on the horizon at various times. This is the key to finding contentment in whatever it is you do. Because doing so requires you to know and internalize that *things are not always going to go your way.* Sometimes they will, and sometimes they won't.

And when they don't, that's okay. God willing, your life will go on.

I want to encourage you to stop living in terms of stop signs and start learning to yield and accelerate. You're going to add years to your life if you can achieve this because you're going to learn how to manage the stressors in your life instead of having *them* rule *you*.

And when we're 100 years old sitting in a rocking chair on the porch watching the sun set, I don't think we're going to be wishing we'd spent more time at the office or on social media. Wishing we'd watched that extra hour of film when we were already prepared for our opponent. Wishing we'd scheduled one more preseason workout even when you knew the team was set for the start of the season.

Instead, if I live to be 100, I hope I will have focused on the 5 "ships" in life:

1. *ownership* in life – owning my decisions and standing by them
2. *craftsmanship* – honing my crafts in coaching, leading, and loving
3. *battleships* – overcoming adversity and learning quickly along the way
4. *championships* – both on the court and otherwise – winning is an everyday thing
5. *relationships* – loving, supporting, and encouraging those around me: the young women I've coached, my friends, and my family

I've listed *relationships* last because I'd argue they're the most important things in life to focus on *getting right.*

Winning championships and building a winning program are obviously important to me, but the wins will fade away in the end. It's the players on the teams I've coached who will stay with me. It's my relationships with former and current assistant coaches. It's my friendships and my bonds with my family members.

Because it's the people that matter. Not the things.

The people.

ROUNDABOUTS
& EXITS

Once you start living your life in terms of yielding and accelerating in and out of roundabouts – as opposed to coming to a screeching halt at stop signs – I think you will find yourself living a more balanced and capable life. Major life events – and even the mundane "every day" – don't need to bring us to our knees. We're human beings, and we were built to withstand trials and tribulations! Doing so requires a disciplined way of living, and learning to yield and accelerate will help you get there.

So, let's dive deeper into what I mean when I refer to life's *roundabouts*.

I mentioned literal roundabouts in an earlier chapter: those road patterns that allow for the flow of vehicles to move around a central circle and then take an exit to move forward on their journey. We'll all been there, and we'll all seen those drivers who know how to operate within one and those who don't!

In life, those roundabouts can mean a variety of things.

When we find ourselves in a roundabout – a transition point that will ultimately lead to something new, depending on which *exit* we take – it could mean we're existing in any of the following situations or scenarios:

1. a stable, content place in our life (ex. you're in a job you really like)
2. a major life event has occurred, and you have to decide what to do next (ex. your long-term relationship ended)
3. a goal (ex. you're working toward becoming head of your department at work)

While some of these scenarios can be fairly straightforward, other roundabouts are more complex and require a lot of contemplation and thoughtfulness on our part. And regardless of the nature of the roundabout you currently find yourself in, there's always the question of: what exit do I take? In other words, *what comes next?*

Because like I've said, navigating a roundabout in the real world requires some skill. You have to know where you're going, and you have to be able to merge with other vehicles and yield in and out of the roundabout. But like I've also said, there's that central lane in the roundabout that allows cars to go around and around.

I remember seeing a video a long time ago of the roundabout at the Arc de Triomphe in Paris, and the filmmakers in this particular video recorded a car going around and around in that center lane for minutes on end. The video is both a little funny and a little sad. Funny because the car goes around in a repetitive motion, but sad because you know that's not what the driver really wants to do. That's an unfulfilling lane to be in, in other words.

So what do we do when we find ourselves having yielded into one of life's roundabouts, and how do we make sure not to get *stuck* in that central lane?

We should start by taking a look at the type of *exits* we often come across in our lifetime. When I say *exits*, I mean things that grab our attention, things that look good, things that we desire and want for ourselves (and in some cases, our families too). These exits can be beneficial or harmful, and deciphering when to take which exit – *if at all* – is part of the art of living.

I'm going to identify and discuss four of the most common and impactful exits I've encountered in my own life: perceived success, money, distractions from the goal, and relationships. They're not the only exits you'll come upon in your lifetime, but they're some of the most common, for sure.

1. *PERCEIVED SUCCESS*

I want to be clear about this particular exit: the keyword here is *perceived*.

Success in and of itself is not an exit. Success is a good thing, and we should all want to achieve success in our own unique way(s). You can also be in a roundabout and find yourself successful (i.e. in a stable job you love), so success itself is not an exit. Feeling successful could stem from a promotion you earned at work, a big sale you made at the company, a case you won in court, or a conference championship you won during the season. These things are objectively successful; they are *successes* and should be celebrated.

Perceived success, however, is an exit that we should avoid.

Perceived success is that feeling we get when we think we've achieved something great *and* we want people to start noticing us for it. In other words, the achievement itself is not enough for many people. There has to be more. And the *more* is often getting recognized or noticed for it.

The moment we let pride creep in and want to have others notice whatever it is we've done…that can be a slippery slope. That can be the wrong exit for so many people. Yes, by taking that exit, you've yielded out of the roundabout. However, in doing so, you've set yourself on an unsustainable path.

Wanting others to notice your success is simply unsustainable.

Maybe for you, perceived success involves driving a fancy car. A car that when people see you drive it makes them think, "Well, she must make a lot of money." Or "He must be really successful to get to drive a car like that." And they're not wrong, but if you start living your life in terms of how *others* view it, that's simply not a healthy or sustainable path.

That is because it will always leave you wanting more. You can't control what others think or feel, right? So say you go out and buy that fancy car because you want people to take notice of you.

What happens when they don't?

What happens when you pull up to that stop sign and want the person next to you to take notice, but they refuse to look your way? Or even worse: they may look over at you and then turn up their nose at you, the guy or girl in the fancy car. Those are all possibilities. And they're all out of your hands. You bought the car with cash wanting to get recognized for it, but people may not have the reaction you want them to have.

Early in my career, I routinely made choices that I thought made the most sense: the choices that would get me to the next step, the next level of coaching. I was an assistant at the D1 and D2 levels, but I obviously wanted to become a Division 1 head coach one day. I did learn a lot when I was working as an assistant. I really did. Yes, I learned a lot about basketball, but I learned things about the type of head coach I would be one day once I got the chance to run a program of my own.

I bring this up now because I also remember as a D1 assistant, the leather chairs on the sideline and the *perception* of what sitting in those chairs meant to me.

Yes, you heard me. The leather chairs.

Take a look at any D1 basketball bench in the country, and they're most likely lined with fancy leather chairs with their school's mascot and/or name on them. I didn't remember chairs like that at the D2 level, so it was new for me at the time. And it was great! It made me feel a certain way. But I got comfortable with it and was more concerned with how it made me look than anything else. It *felt* fancy, and that's what I cared about in many ways at the time. How I looked. How others perceived me.

So while *perceived success* might look like an attractive exit, don't take it! Stay in that roundabout until you come upon an exit that makes the most sense for *you*. And the *perceived success* exit is not the one.

2. *MONEY*

Money's often a touchy subject, right?

Unless you're one of those people who truly live off the grid and grow your own food, we all need money to survive.

So this is not an exit that can be totally avoided. There may be times in your life when you have to take that exit – a change of careers or a promotion that comes with a higher salary – in order to provide for yourself and your family. In those cases, I would encourage you to take that exit. However, there are many times when the *money* exit is simply not the one for you.

I'm talking about the times when we're tempted to think that money is the answer to all our problems. As in, *if I only made $10,000 more, I'd really be set.*

Or, *all my friends make $100k, and I want that too.*

Or, *my company doesn't value me as an employee because I'm underpaid.*

I'm willing to bet that a lot of us have felt those feelings or have had those thoughts at some point in our lives. And I don't think any of these sentiments are wrong, exactly. I mean, there were definitely times in my own career when I thought I was underpaid. I think that's a very relatable thing: to recognize our own value and want our employer to recognize that same value, but on the dotted line. That's normal in a lot of ways.

But what's not normal – and when you should not take the *money* exit – is when you find yourself thinking that your salary is the only thing that matters. That money is the end all, be all of life on Earth. Those are the times when that *money* exit is going to look really good. You're coming up on it in the roundabout and you find yourself thinking, *This is the answer for me.*

I promise you. It is not the answer.

I'm sure many of you have heard the old adage of "find something you love in life, figure out a way to get paid for it, and you'll never work a day in your life." Find the joy; then comes the money, right? Words like those don't stick around forever if there's no meaning behind them. They're spot-on in a lot of ways. But the thing is, a lot of us do not have the luxury of loving the work we do.

I'm fortunate that I do, in fact, love my job. Can't imagine doing anything else.

But I'm lucky to feel that way.

A lot of people have jobs they hate, and the money is the only reason they're doing it. And the concept of earning more money may mean they hop around and pursue this job or that job, or take on multiple jobs simultaneously in order to make more money. Some of these people *have* to have multiple jobs in order to make ends meet, and I commend them for their hard work. I know that lifestyle can't be easy.

But I also know a lot of people who take on various jobs because making money is their primary interest. They're not interested in the work. They have zero passion for it. They're only interested when that paycheck hits their bank account.

But guess what? That feeling? That rush of dopamine when they see those numbers go up in their bank account? That feeling is fleeting. It's here one moment and gone the next.

And that's my point about the *money* exit. It's another unsustainable exit.

Because there's always more money to be made. There's always another deal to close, another sale to make. There are billionaires out there who are not happy.

In other words, with money, *there's never enough*.

So if we make major life decisions with money as the only goal in mind, we are going to be sorely disappointed when it's never enough.

If you want to take that new job with a higher salary because you love the work, then do it! You *should* take it! Those are not the instances I'm referring to with regard to the *money* exit. I'm talking about those times when we see the *money* exit as the solution coming around the bend and find ourselves thinking that that's the exit with all the right answers.

It may look shiny – and it has looked shiny to me several times in my own life and career – but there's no substance there. There's nothing to back it up. You'll find yourself unfulfilled if money is your number one goal in life.

So to play off of that adage I mentioned earlier: if you can find a line of work you love, then you're one of the lucky ones. But don't chase that bottom line. It will only leave you wanting more, and you'll find yourself right back where you started from more times than not.

3. DISTRACTIONS FROM THE GOAL

Here's an easier one to discuss because this exit is always a bad idea! No confusion involved, people. Avoid this exit at all costs.

One of the mantras I live by is this: Issues and drama are simply a distraction from the goal.

Truer words have never been spoken, in my humble opinion.

There are also so many things that qualify as distractions, and they should all be avoided. I'll only mention some of them here, but I'm sure you can come up with many others if you use your imagination.

If you find yourself checking your phone or tablet a dozen (or more) times a day to look at social media: that's a distraction.

If you're a people pleaser who finds yourself doing lots of things simply so that others will like you: distraction.

If you check in with certain friends only to gossip about your other friends: distraction.

Online gambling: distraction.

Spending hours a day online shopping: distraction.

Watching four seasons of a show on Netflix in a week: distraction.

Pornography: distraction.

The list goes on and on.

Anything that serves to shift your attention from your goal – consciously or subconsciously – is a distraction, and you have to eliminate as many of those as you can from your life.

But the tough part is this: we often find ourselves in vulnerable moments in life, many of which qualify as one of those roundabouts I've been referring to, and things that qualify as distractions often appear to be fun. We often justify taking part in them because we're only having fun. Or we want to treat ourselves for a hard day, or a hard week, or a hard month.

Therefore, oftentimes when we round that bend in the roundabout and see something seemingly fun up ahead, we take the exit.

But the exit itself is a distraction, and when we take it, we find ourselves out of the roundabout and on a path that's not going to move us forward in the right direction.

As I've said before, I'm not perfect nor do I pretend to be. I've taken the *distractions* exit many times, and many times, it has left me unfulfilled and further behind in my goals. Because that's all they are! Yes, certain distractions can look innocent from the outside, but the end results leave you further behind on your goals.

Remember I talked about the habits of the 3% earlier? Well, the 3% *do not let themselves be distracted.* They are *relentless* about it. They've trained themselves to recognize those *distraction* exits and avoid them 100% of the time. This is partly what makes them elite performers. They're so focused on their decades-long desires and goals that the threat of a distraction is simply that: a threat. It's not a reality for them because they don't play that game.

So over the course of time, you have to train yourself to recognize distractions for what they are and avoid them at all costs. The 97% let distractions play a major role in their lives, but you don't have to! You want to be one of the 3%! Stay focused and keep your eyes on the road ahead.

4. *RELATIONSHIPS*

In my humble opinion, the most important exit you'll ever come across is the *relationships* exit. And this one's another tricky one because it can be both a good one – you choosing a relationship that sustains you and builds you up – or a bad one, in which you choose a relationship that you know is toxic and unhealthy.

While I do know some people out there who are convinced they'll never find true love or have no interest in doing so, the vast majority of people I know – myself included – want to find that one "teammate" to spend the rest of their life with. And while that can be a wonderful thing to be a part of – a long-term relationship with the love of your life – it can be really difficult getting there for a lot of people.

Dating is harder now than ever before. Even though modern technology brings many people together in more ways than ever before, I think we live in a society that's very disconnected and disjointed. The pandemic certainly didn't help the matter. It quite literally separated people for months and then years. So my hat is off to everyone out there reading this book who currently finds himself or herself in the dating pool. It can be rough out there!

That's often why the *relationships* exit looks so attractive.

Many of us have found ourselves in that roundabout looking for the right exit to take us to our next destination in life, and the *relationships* exit is often the shiniest exit out there. It can look *really* good. But if you find yourself taking that exit, it doesn't always mean it's the right exit for you.

We all know some people who are in toxic relationships. Relationships that are unhealthy, unsustainable, and often abusive. But at first, those same relationships probably looked pretty good. That's why each party got involved in the first place. *Things looked good* at the start. They often do.

But finding the right person or even finding the right people to date can be an incredible challenge. If we view it in terms of having one shot to get it right and make it count, we should *embrace* the time, energy, and effort it takes to discern whether or not to enter into a relationship. There's often lots of heartache along the way as we experience rejection, lose someone we really like, or even lose a part of ourselves in the process. Many people want to avoid all these emotions and the heartache at all costs, so they choose this exit because they want to be loved. However, they've chosen the exit for the wrong person. Oftentimes, people don't know they're making the wrong choice in a partner because as I've said, things often look really good at the start.

But sometimes, however, people knowingly enter a relationship with the wrong partner simply because they don't want to be alone anymore. Or they want to have what everyone else has. Or they want children, and the only way to get there is to settle down with a partner. I can't blame these people for wanting to feel love because that's a universal concept. But so many people out there chase the *wrong* people. We've all seen it before. Maybe we've even done some of the chasing. These people see the *relationships* exit and take it without considering if it's really the best decision for them in the long run.

I want to encourage people reading this book to take a good, long look at the *relationships* exit the next time you come upon one in your life. (People currently in a relationship: good luck, and I hope you're both in it for the right reasons!) When you see that exit and you know there's a viable option out there for you to pursue in a committed relationship, you need to ask yourself a few questions. Is this relationship going to sustain me? Is it going to bring me closer to God? Is it going to complement me the same way in which I complement the other person?

You must also take stock of *yourself* because in order to be the best *we*, you first have to be the best *you*.

I'm not saying that you'll always have the answers to these questions, nor will you always get it right. We've all made mistakes with our romantic relationships, I would bet. But I'm simply encouraging you to take stock of the situation and make as informed a decision as possible. I know that may sound very technical, and I don't want you to ignore your gut feelings or what your heart is telling you to do.

Keep in mind that simply because you see the *relationships* exit approaching, you do not have to take it! You can't pick your family, but you can pick whom you choose to marry. Choose wisely!

In closing, while I haven't gone over all of the types of exits you may encounter in your lifetime, I've attempted to touch upon some of the most common. The tricky part with exits is that many of them – if not all of them – often look really good. And we might find ourselves feeling a bit of FOMO (Fear of Missing Out) if we don't take a certain exit.

But I want to encourage you to take your time when you find yourself in one of life's roundabouts.

Take. Your. Time.

An informed decision that took you months to make is better than an uninformed one you make in 10 seconds, a decision that is now leaving you unfulfilled and hopeless.

This is a reminder too that we often make "business decisions" to leave or exit certain things in life – a marriage, a job, a living situation – but rarely do we make the same "business decisions" when entering into something. So whether you're entering a certain roundabout or looking for the right exit out of one, take your time. Take your time and train yourself to take the exit that makes the most sense *for you*. It will take lots of practice and self-reflection, but I know you can do it.

JENNI'S STORY, PART ONE

As the players and staff – the *team* – took that charter bus home to Greensboro on that cold, bright Saturday morning in February, I knew that the bumbling nature of the ride was bound to put me to sleep as soon as I sat down. The emotional exhaustion of the previous 24 hours hit me as soon as I took my seat, but I knew I couldn't sleep. At least, not right away. My brain wouldn't quit yet because there was plenty to think about.

My phone was full of text messages and voicemails, but there would be time for all that soon enough. I turned it off and put it inside my bag. I closed my eyes as I sat in the plush seat on the bus, steadying my breathing to center myself. We had a few hours until we would arrive in Greensboro, and I wanted to use a lot of that time to reflect.

The game itself was playing on a loop in my head. I've always had a steel trap for a brain when it comes to a basketball game: remembering individual possessions, defensive sequences, turning points in the game, officials' calls, substitutions, all of it. In many ways, this is a blessing. I can reflect on a game before there's even time to cut film.

But it's also a curse.

Reliving a game in your mind is great when you win. A loss, however, is vastly different. Everything that went wrong replays itself over and over, and you're at its mercy for how long that feeling may last.

As I sat there on the bus, eyes closed, thinking, questions started to creep into my mind.

How was that game over so quickly?

How was the *season* over?

This was such a special group – I was coaching at my alma mater, for heaven's sake – and we'd been having such a great year. Up until 24 hours prior, we'd been 25-1 and ready to play in the NCAA tournament.

At the present moment, however, I was on a bus headed home. Someone else would win. Someone other than us.

I kept asking myself these questions about our season as I continued to replay certain moments from the game in my mind. With my phone turned off and in my bag, I lost track of time.

At one point, I leaned my head over and opened my eyes to stare out the window. We were on a backroad at the time, and the bus was flying through the mountains. The air outside was crisp and the sun was bright, almost like early fall, even though we were in the tail end of winter and heading into spring.

And although we'd come to the end of our season – a stop sign – I attempted to think about the renewal of things as those fields of green flew by. I attempted to ground my emotions by activating different senses, a strategy I encourage the team and those I work with on EQ to employ as they see fit. As I sat on the bus, I decided I should probably listen to a guided meditation to center myself and not dwell on the negativity of our season having ended. I was also drinking some water with a hint of grapefruit juice, a scent and flavor I use to focus my energy and mind.

Those things certainly helped, but it's tough because the nature of a college sports season – no matter the level, no matter the sport – can be the most intense few months of your year. And if you're not learning to acquire that *yielding* sensibility that I spoke of earlier in this book, the end of the season can bring you to a screeching halt.

I'd been there before.

I've lost that last game, whether it be in the regular season or the postseason, and have had the abruptness of that final loss bring me to my knees many times.

Think about it. You go from the intensity of the season – focused on developing players, building team chemistry, and *winning* – to the next day being a regular day.

No practice plan to write.

No scouting report to create.

No team meetings.

This abruptness has been incredibly difficult for me to deal with in the past. However, I've come to a point in my life where I am no longer living in a stop-and-go mindset.

I had yielded and accelerated *into* this particular season, and I would soon yield *out* of it.

That's not to say that yielding nullifies the pain you may be feeling at the end of the season. It certainly does not. I was on that bus in *pain*, to a degree.

But you can train yourself – like I did – to learn that when a *season* of your life is over, this does not mean that your entire life comes to a halt. It merely means you're moving into the next season of your life, one with its own unique opportunities.

In my case, the next *season* would be postseason work, individual workouts, exit meetings, etc. The things that all college coaches do once their respective seasons are over. But it would also mean spending time working on my relationships outside of basketball. Spending more time with family and friends. Nurturing those relationships and friendships. For those outside the coaching profession, this applies to you, as well.

In a teacher's life, that may mean yielding into the summer – that time of year when you recharge for the following school year.

In a doctor's life, that may mean scheduling a two-week vacation after several months of intense surgeries.

In a politician's life, it may mean regrouping after an election loss and gearing up for the next election cycle after some downtime with family.

Sometimes, we have to retreat in order to plan our next *attack*, in other words.

So as I continued to stare out at the beautiful landscape going by as we ventured home on the bus, I was thinking about all these things.

The different seasons of life.

The nature of change and how it's unavoidable.

Reinterpreting life's stop signs as *roundabouts* instead.

Yielding within life's roundabouts, deciphering which exit ramp to take, and then accelerating into the next stage of life.

I closed my eyes again, but as I did, I felt the bus come to a stop.

I opened my eyes dreamily and looked out the window. We were at a four-way stop, and there was a car dealership across from us. It was bright outside, and I was forced to squint to really get a good look. As I looked out, I swore to myself that I saw someone I knew.

Is that Jenni? I thought to myself, sitting up in my seat to get a better look.

I squinted and leaned forward, forehead touching the glass of the window.

The young woman I was looking at was walking down a row of cars with a young man I didn't recognize.

Is it? I continued to ask myself. I had been her college coach years ago, but I hadn't seen her in quite some time. It did look like her, but with so much time having passed, she might have changed her look. It was certainly possible. I looked more closely.

It could *be Jenni. That's so cool that she's looking for a new car! And that's actually my friend Passion Poindexter's car lot, so I know she'll get the deal of a lifetime like I did.*

With the sun shining so brightly, I leaned back and closed my eyes again. I started to reminisce about Jenni and my life back then.

While we're on the subject, let me tell you about her.

Jenni's Story, Part One

Her nickname is Jenni "One-Shot" Andrews. I know. A bit odd, right?

She's a twenty-something former college basketball player from the United States. She got that nickname on the court because she typically only needed one shot to make a basket. She graduated college with a 98% career field goal percentage (because, hey, nobody's perfect). She spent her college years driven by achieving great things in the classroom and on the court, and she graduated *summa cum laude* with a degree in Business. Jenni has always had a lot to be proud of.

At present, Jenni One-Shot has recently landed her dream job in a sprawling city in the southeastern United States. She's the head of her department at a big non-profit downtown, and she's looking to get settled into her new life. She thinks she's found a good fit with a church right around the corner from her new apartment. She also has a good friend from college who lives nearby named Johnny Cooper.

He's also a former college athlete, and they

got to know each other through the athletics department at their school. He's been a reliable friend to her over the years when other people in her life have come and gone. In college, their friends always thought they were dating, but they've never taken it that far. They've been great friends for years, and that's been all.

With regard to Jenni's present situation, she's familiar with the city – her new home – and she's aware that it lacks reliable public transportation. She'll need a car to get around. When we see her on this particular day on the car lot, she and Johnny are there for Jenni to possibly get a new car. She's done a little research online, and this seems to be the best car dealership out there.

Miles of cars, trucks, and SUVs recede into the distance, and the light shining off the thousands of windshields is practically blinding. The lot is packed with people, but Jenni and Johnny are still able to move around pretty easily and see what they want. Johnny's tried to talk to her ahead of time about the most important things you need to keep in mind when buying a new car, but Jenni has basically shrugged off those conversations. She's not sure exactly what she wants – a sports car, a sedan, an SUV, or even a truck – but she'll know it when she sees it. She's had that sort of confidence about her for her entire life, and this time is no different.

As Jenni walks ahead toward a row of sedans, Johnny trails behind her, squinting into the distance. He sees a woman walking toward them. Even from a distance, he can see that she is smiling from ear to ear.

"Jenni," Johnny says in a forceful whisper. "Someone's coming."

Jenni looks up.

"Helloooo," the woman says cheerily from a distance. Even amidst the excitement of the lot filled with people, they can hear her as clear as day.

"Do you know her?" Johnny whispers out of the side of his mouth.

"No," Jenni whispers back.

As the woman comes closer, they can see that she is a tall black woman who appears to be in her 40s or 50s, wearing a blazer with matching heels. Her smile and demeanor immediately draw Jenni and Johnny forward.

"Hello! Good morning!" Johnny says, walking toward the woman.

"Hi!" Jenni says, walking over.

They find themselves standing together under a tree to shade them from the sun.

"Good morning! I'm Passion Poindexter, and I'm the owner of this here car lot." She swings one arm out wide to take in the sweeping views of the lot and its multiple vast sections. "Welcome!"

"Thank you so much," Jenni says, shaking her hand. "I've recently moved to the area, and I'm looking to-"

"I'm sorry, my girl. I wasn't finished. Ahem," she says, clearing her throat. "I was about to say that I saw you from across the way, and I wanted to say that I'm so glad you're here. Really, I am. But unfortunately, I can't sell you a car."

"Huh?" Jenni and Johnny say simultaneously, looking at one another.

"Allow me to explain. I said I can't *sell* you a car today. I *own* this car lot, so I can happily give you one."

Jenni's jaw drops.

"Give me one?"

She looks at Johnny, who is clearly as confused as she is.

Johnny's typically the rock in Jenni's life, and the fact that he is also confused leaves her immediately uneasy. Ever since they first met in college when he was a sophomore on the men's basketball team and Jenni a freshman on the women's team, they had each been the person the other one could count on through thick and thin. Sure, they argued every so often, but they were incredibly close. Johnny knows that Jenni wants his help in this whole business of getting a new car, but Passion's words at the moment are bewildering. He shrugs his shoulders to confirm his feelings to Jenni.

"Sure! I'm in charge! And every so often, a customer comes along who has that special...something. And you've got it, my dear."

"Well, thank you. Really. I don't really know what to say," Jenni says.

"I can see it in your eyes. A spark. A kindness. A driven ambition. It's what made me walk over here when there are a hundred other customers I could be engaging with at the moment," Passion says matter-of-factly.

Jenni looks down at the ground.

"Thank you, Passion," she says quietly.

Passion looks at Johnny and says, "I understand that this is a lot to take in at one time. So while you're already overwhelmed, let me also say there's a catch!"

Jenni and Johnny look at each other again.

"A catch?" Jenni says.

"Yes, a catch. You can pick any car on this lot, absolutely any one you like, regardless of price. But you'll need to have the mindset to drive it for the rest of your life."

"Excuse me?"

"You heard me, my dear. You must choose wisely because you only get one shot."

A shiver runs down Jenni's spine. She looks at Johnny.

"My nickname's Jenni-"

"One-Shot. I know," Passion says.

"How do you-" Johnny starts to say, but Passion is already talking again and walking away.

"So walk around with your friend here. Johnny, right?" Passion looks over her shoulder.

Johnny gulps.

"Yes?!" he says. *She knows my name!*, he thinks.

"Right, so walk around with Johnny, and think long and hard about it. There are new and used. Sedans, trucks, SUVs, minivans. All different types of engines, transmissions, upgrades, trim levels, you name it. Too many options, really. But you need to choose wisely because like I said, you'll be driving it for the rest of your life. There's *zero* exit strategy here, people. No Plans B, or C, or D...This car will be the one for you. Forever..."

Passion says all this, moving her arms again to capture the expanse of the lot as she walks away from the two friends.

"Forever..." Jenni says, trailing off.

She takes a deep breath, and she and Johnny start to walk around, soon disappearing into the crowd.

Jenni has been charged with a monumental task: to make a decision that will potentially affect the rest of her life, and she's only got one chance to get it right.

She and Johnny are about to undertake this task together, and they're bound to ask themselves a million questions about Jenni's circumstances. This is about her present, her future, her goals, her dreams – and even her past. All of this matters when making decisions. Where we've been, where we are, where we're going.

In Jenni's case, these are all great questions. And sure, objectively, some cars are better than others, depending on any given criteria. But when it's about *you* and the right fit, no single car is better than any other one. It's about finding what works for *you*, what feels right, what will take you to your next destination in life, quite literally.

So as Passion walks off into the distance, Jenni and Johnny start down a row of SUVs. Jenni touches a blue sporty-looking one on the end of a row.

"Ow!" she says, sticking her finger in her mouth. "It's so hot!" she says.

"Be careful," Johnny says. "If there's one you really like, we'll get Passion to give us the keys for a test drive. We can crank the A/C," he says."

"A test drive? I'm not even thinking about that yet. I don't even know what kind of car I want!"

"Not at all?" Johnny asks.

"Not really. I mean, I know what I need it to do. I live in a city, right? So a car that gets good gas mileage and is conservative in stop-and-go traffic makes sense."

"True," Johnny says. "Do you think you'll do much traveling for your job?"

"I don't think so. But I guess I don't really know yet. I'm sure there are lots of things about the job that I have yet to learn," Jenni says.

"Right. And I hate to remind you, but Passion did say that you'll be driving whichever car you choose for the rest of your life. So maybe choose one that serves a variety of purposes?"

Jenni looks off into the distance.

"Maybe…" she says.

She spots a sports car in the next row that she likes the look of.

"Ooo! Look at that one!" she points and is off running, Johnny trailing behind.

Jenni speeds off, and Johnny has to sprint to catch up. When he does, Jenni's got her hands on her knees sucking air.

"This one. This is it," she says, out of breath.

He sees that she's standing in front of a blue sports car, but he notices that it's also a hybrid.

"Huh," he says, slowly walking around the car. "This one?"

"This one," she says, standing upright. "Look at it! It's beautiful! It'll be so fun to drive, and I'll save money on gas because it's a hybrid."

"Hmm…I don't know…" Johnny says, bending over to see inside.

"Well!" a voice yells.

"Ahhh!" scream Jenni and Johnny in unison. They turn. It's Passion.

"Oooo, I'm sorry to scare you like that, but I saw you both running and thought I'd come take a look."

"It's okay. I'm glad you're here," Jenni says.

"So, you think you want this beauty," Passion says, smiling.

"Yes, I think this is the one. I have a gut instinct about it."

"Would you like to take it for a spin?" Passion asks. "You know, this *will* be your car for the rest of your life."

"Sure, sure. Yes, you need to test drive it, Jenni," Johnny says.

"I don't need to!" Jenni says excitedly. "This is the one!"

"What?!" Johnny screams.

"You're positive?" Passion asks.

"Positive," Jenni says.

"Shouldn't you think on it? Pray about it?" Johnny asked intently. He knows how much her relationship with God means to her. That she has a rich prayer life.

"I don't think I need to," she says.

"This is a bad idea," Johnny says, shaking his head.

"Oh please, relax," Jenni says, practically jumping up and down.

"Okay, here we go," Passion says with a wave of her hand. A single sheet of white paper appears in her hand, and she pulls out a pen from behind her ear. "I need your John Hancock," she says.

Jenni sets the paper down on the roof of the car and signs it with a flourish. She turns to Passion and hands it back to her. As she does so, she hears the tinkling of keys as they hit her open palm. The car is hers.

When we next see Jenni, she's been driving her new hybrid sports car for several weeks, and she's loving it.

She's saving money on gas because it gets such good mileage, and the car can hold a lot of her work materials and her bike on weekends. Johnny and his tall frame fit nicely in the passenger seat, and he even finds himself wanting to drive it from time to time. That is, when Jenni lets him.

On this particular day when she's driving, she stops to get gas at the corner store but first heads inside to get a drink. A sweet tea, maybe. When she opens the door, the chiming of the tiny bell hanging above the door marks her arrival. She's in front of the cold case of drinks, peering through the frosted glass, when the woman next to her speaks.

"Hi," the woman says, and Jenni turns. The woman is roughly the same height and build as Jenni, with the same hairstyle. She's also wearing clothes that Jenni might have picked out herself. But she appears to be at least twenty years older than Jenni. Mid-40s, probably.

"Hi," Jenni says, smiling.

"That you in the hybrid out there?" the woman says, pointing with her thumb outside.

"Yep, that's me! Got it a few weeks ago," Jenni says proudly.

"I love that kind of car! Had one like it years ago," she says.

"Oh, really?"

"Yep, great car. Traded it in for something bigger after we started having children."

"That makes sense. That's nice you've got kids. I'm Jenni, by the way," she says as she holds out her hand, wanting to make a friend.

The woman shakes it.

"I'm Autumn," she says.

"Beautiful name," Jenni says, looking at her. As she does, she notices something in Autumn's eyes. "I'm sorry, but have you been crying?" Jenni asks.

"I have been, yes," Autumn says, rubbing her eyes a bit. "I can't believe I'm saying this, but I'm divorced and it was finalized as of yesterday."

"Oh, I'm so sorry," Jenni says, touching Autumn's elbow.

Autumn starts to get choked up. "Here, let's go outside," Jenni says. She leads Autumn out of the store, and they sit down across from each other at a picnic table outside the store under a big umbrella.

"I'm sorry for being emotional with a stranger at a gas station!" Autumn says.

"Don't apologize at all! This is a very vulnerable time for you, I imagine."

"It is," Autumn says. "It really is. It's a happy time because it's something I wanted, but the finality of it has made me very emotional."

She pauses.

"But I'm taking it one day at a time and thinking about the positives."

"That's a great strategy," Jenni says. "May I ask about your kids?"

"Sure!" Autumn says, and then pauses. "Tommy and Lucinda. Twins actually. They're 14."

"Oh my goodness! That's so cool. Twins! And what an age…right on the cusp of being teenagers. You couldn't pay me a million dollars to go back to that age," Jenni says.

"Tell me about it! They're wonderful, to be honest, and I'm not only saying that because they're mine. They get good grades and play sports. And Tommy plays the oboe. Luci does ballet," Autumn says.

"That's amazing," Jenni says. "So you have them to hold on to during this time."

"Yes," Autumn says, "I do. I count on them, for sure. The thing that makes me saddest about all this is that they won't be growing up in a house that has two parents. I feel like I've let them down in a major way."

"Well, not knowing much about your situation, I'm sure your children don't blame you for the divorce. I would think they're old enough to understand what's going on, at least to some degree."

"They are; they're definitely old enough to know what's going on. Or at least as much as they *should* know. We weren't a couple that really fought all that much, especially not in front of the kids. We sort of...fell out of love. And it was devastating."

"I can imagine," Jenni says. "Do you have a faith life that you find support in?"

"I do, thank goodness," Autumn says. "I'm a pretty active member of my church, and the kids go to Youth Group with their friends. I'm lucky," she says.

"That's awesome! I have found such comfort in my church group over the years. It's only been a short while, but I already feel so welcome at my new church. I'm glad to hear that you have a similar situation. It's so important," Jenni says.

"You're absolutely right," Autumn says. Then, she looks down at Jenni's hands that are folded on the table.

"You don't have a wedding ring on. Are you dating anyone?"

Jenni laughs softly.

"No, I'm not. There's...always been someone in the back of my mind, but we make better friends than anything else," Jenni says.

"I completely understand. Friends are important too," Autumn says.

"And speaking of friends, do you have people close to you to help you along through all this? Other than your kids?"

"I do. I certainly do. I'm blessed with a small but mighty friend group. They've already threatened to slash his tires, but I asked them not to as I bought the car he drives now and I still like it," Autumn says as she and Jenni share a laugh.

"Well, your friends sound great."

"They are. And I'm actually looking forward to what the next phase of my life holds, to be honest. Yes, my marriage failed, but I can't look at it as *I* failed. A marriage is a two-way street, and I cannot blame myself for everything that happened. So I'm not going to wallow in self-pity or go down a weird path where I feel sorry for myself and refuse to get out of bed or leave the house. I can't do that to myself. I can't do that to my children," Autumn says.

"If I may be frank, you're being very positive and mature about the whole thing," Jenni says.

"Well, I'm forty-five, so I better be mature about it," Autumn says, laughing.

"Sure, but in all seriousness, I know some people whose divorce essentially comes to define them for a long, long time, and not in a good way," Jenni says.

"I know some of those people also. And as I was going through this, I kept thinking to myself that I could not become one of them. I could not let the *challenge* of my divorce bring about the end of my livelihood forever."

"That's great thinking!" Jenni says.

"Like I said, I'm forty-five. But forty-five doesn't mean I'm dead! I still have hope for finding love again somewhere out there if that's what's in the cards for me. Overall, I need to decide what's next for me. And I'm going to take my time figuring it out," Autumn says, standing up. "I've already told you way too much as a complete stranger, but thank you so much for taking the time to chat with me."

Jenni gets up, as well, and moves around to the same side of the picnic bench as Autumn.

"Of course, of course. I'm sorry I caught you at a vulnerable moment back in there," Jenni says, pointing her thumb at the convenience store.

"Don't worry about it one bit. I'm happy to have met you," Autumn says.

"I'm happy about that, as well." Jenni says. The two women hug and exchange phone numbers. "Good luck with everything. Let me know if I can ever help," she says.

"Thanks, you too," Autumn says. "And that friend you were talking about earlier?"

Jenni thinks of Johnny.

"Yeah?" Jenni asks.

"Sometimes, the greatest life partner starts out as a friend. Don't rule it out," Autumn says and winks, walking away.

"Huh," Jenni says aloud, even though Autumn is gone.

Jenni goes back in to pay for her gas, and she's off.

Autumn has taught Jenni a powerful lesson.

Autumn is dealing with an all-too-common hurdle in modern life – divorce from one's life partner – and yet she's making a conscious decision and effort to not let it cripple her. That doesn't mean she's not upset. Heck, Jenni finds her practically crying in the corner store. Of course, she's upset! She used to love her spouse very much! But what she's not doing is wallowing in that pain and despair. She's not letting that pain bring her life to a screeching halt.

Life's thrown a stop sign at her, but she's refusing to stop.

Instead, she's *choosing* to feel her feelings while also looking forward.

She's *choosing* to yield and accelerate into the next phase of her life, whatever that may mean for her. She has found herself in one of life's roundabouts, and she's choosing her next exit wisely. Those who choose wisely also sleep soundly, and Autumn is making choices that will bring her some sound sleep, in other words. She knows that bad things happen in life, but that doesn't mean that life stops or that it's any less worth living. She can be distraught over the end of her marriage while also being excited about what comes next. *She can do both.* Grieving any type of loss is different for everyone, and it's not necessarily mutually exclusive to other feelings and desires.

We as human beings are complex creatures who can feel a variety of emotions at once.

Therefore, a stop sign doesn't have to mean the end of the world. We can feel sadness or grief while also putting one foot in front of the other and moving forward. We can feel sadness and grief *while also feeling* joy.

Autumn is yielding at a time when that type of attitude and way of thinking can be incredibly helpful. And she is not ignoring her pain, but rather, she's embracing it and allowing it to fuel her next phase of life.

She is not moving *on*, but moving forward.

She's paving her path forward with the green bricks of friendship and family.

She will wait for the right exit to come around, and then she will accelerate confidently into the next stage of life.

And as Jenni drives out of the corner store's parking lot and heads down the road, she starts to relive her conversation with Autumn.

A woman who's been through so much – and is going through so much *right now* –is choosing to keep her head up and continue to live her life. *That kind of perseverance and grit is inspiring*, Jenni thinks.

Something Autumn said specifically keeps replaying itself in Jenni's head:

"I'm going to take my time," Autumn had said.

Take my time...Jenni thinks.

Another thought creeps into her mind.

I should have gotten an SUV, she thinks. *Dang it!*

She pulls a U-turn at the next exit and calls Johnny on the phone, frantic.

"Johnny!" she screams as soon as he picks up.

"Jenni? Are you okay?" he says.

"I made a mistake!" she screams. "Meet me back at the car lot. Now!"

When they both arrive at the lot, Passion is already walking toward them.

"What's going on? I didn't expect to see the two of you again so soon," Passion says as Jenni and Johnny park and get out. She's looking as good as ever in another matching pantsuit and heels.

"I've made a mistake," Jenni says.

"A mistake?!" Passion asks, genuinely in shock.

"Yes!"

"But I told you that you'd only have one chance to make this decision and that you'd have to stick to it. There's no exit strategy, remember?"

"I remember! That's why I'm freaking out," Jenni says as Johnny pulls her in for a hug.

"It's okay," he says, "We'll figure this out. I've got your back."

"Come along," Passion says, motioning for Jenni to follow her. Jenni and Johnny lock eyes, and he motions for her to go ahead. Jenni walks up to Passion, and they start walking off together.

"So you've made a mistake, you say," Passion says, walking away and looking off into the distance. "Jenni, I'd like to talk to you alone." Jenni walks ahead to catch up with her.

"I want to tell you: I'm disappointed in you," Passion says.

This stings more than Jenni anticipated it would because she hasn't known Passion for that long, but the woman's opinion already means a lot to her.

"I know," Jenni says. "I'm so sorry."

"I understand you're sorry, but you have to understand. I made a deal with you the other day, and I thought you understood the terms of that deal."

"I did," Jenni says.

"Well apparently, you didn't. Because you're back here already and want to switch cars. Isn't your nickname 'One-Shot'?"

"It is," Jenni says.

"So where's that girl? The one who shot 98% from the field in college?"

"How'd you know-"

"I'm friends with your college coach. She told me all about you," Passion says.

"I see," Jenni says.

"So what happened to *that* Jenni? That young woman would have made the right choice the first time around. She had confidence," Passion says.

"Well, I hate to tell you, but apparently I'm not that girl anymore. People change. *I've* changed, I suppose. I wouldn't say drastically, but am I the same person I was in college? Heck no," Jenni says.

"Tell me more about that," Passion says as they turn down another row of cars.

"There's not much to tell really. I think that a person evolves over time; at least I did. I *like* the person I was in college, but that version of me was very naïve about how the world worked. That Jenni didn't have much to worry about, to be honest. She focused on two things: school and basketball. And if something didn't fall into one of those two categories, she didn't bother with it. I miss it in some ways because life was simpler back then."

"It often is when we're younger. 'Ignorance is bliss' didn't become a cliché for no good reason," Passion says.

"Exactly!" Jenni says. "*That* Jenni lived in ignorance in a lot of ways. But today, sheesh. The world is a crazy place. Ignorance is inexcusable."

"That it is," Passion says. "And with that being said, that also means that our decisions have consequences. You should have taken your time and made a more informed decision. Sure, a gut feeling about something is important, but some things in life require more deliberation. Especially considering I said there was no exit strategy. You have to be two feet in," Passion says. "You've got to learn something from all this. The real world is going to be much less forgiving than I am, Jenni. And life is only going to present so many learning opportunities to you. You'll miss the whole point if you don't pay attention when they come around."

"I feel you," Jenni says. "When's the last time you experienced one of those moments?"

"Actually, it wasn't too long ago. I was faced with needing to fire someone on my staff who was not pulling his weight."

"How so?" Jenni asks as they turn down another row, heading back toward Johnny.

"Well, he works in the sales office. Name's Donovan. And he's a good salesman, really vibrant young man. But he was coming in late, leaving early, those types of things. And the other staff members were taking notice and weren't too happy."

"Did you fire him?"

"I thought about it, sure," Passion says. "Firing him would have been the easy route because it could have been over in about 10 minutes, and then I wouldn't have had to worry about him anymore. But I tried to get to the root of why he was shirking some of his responsibilities around here. At the end of the day, he's a good salesman and a nice guy, so I didn't want to let him go if I didn't have to," Passion says.

"So what happened?"

"I confronted him when he came in thirty minutes late one morning, and we had a heart-to-heart. Turns out he'd been going through a lot with his girlfriend, and they were in the process of having a baby. Had some issues. So, he'd been staying up super late attempting to work things out with her, and he'd also been leaving early some days to go to IVF appointments with her. When he told me this, I cried," Passion says.

"I don't blame you. That's a lot," Jenni says.

"But it was great because I was able to see things from his perspective, and it completely altered my decision to fire him. I'm letting him come in an hour later than the other salespeople for awhile, but he's staying an hour later than them also. And he's got to request time off for the appointments and not leave early anymore," Passion says.

"You're really nice to do that for him," Jenni says.

"He's part of the team, Jenni, and I like to take care of people on the team. That includes you. So when you asked me when's the last time the universe presented me with a moment that requires me to pay attention and learn something, I told the story about Donovan. But what I'm recognizing right now is that I'm also in one of those moments as we speak," Passion says, stopping to turn to Jenni.

Jenni stops and smiles at Passion. Her new friend.

"I want to help you. I don't simply want to take the car back and have you go on your merry way. I want you to learn from this. You know, I'm a nice person who can be very forgiving. The real world out there? Not so much," Passion says, taking Jenni's hand.

"I can see that. And I will learn from this. I promise," Jenni says as they start walking again, hand in hand. By this time, they've come upon Johnny who's peering into another car's window. He sees them and stands up.

"I should have taken more time to make a decision, Passion. I think I should have gone with an SUV. More rugged, more durable. Room for an expanded family. I wasn't thinking far enough into the future when I decided on the hybrid. I might have a family one day, right? I'll need three rows for our kids and all our stuff."

"*Our* kids?" Johnny says.

"Oh hush, you know what I mean! That car could get me anywhere and help me haul anything that needs hauling. Johnny, you love yours, right?"

"I do," he says, "I do. But I'm not you!"

"I know," Jenni says. "I know. I think I rushed it and didn't make a wise choice."

Passion turns and walks back toward them.

"Well, to be honest, you're not the first person who's made a mistake on my lot," she says.

"I'm not?" Jenni asks.

"No, you're not. It's unfortunate, but it's happened before."

"I see…" Jenni says, silently hoping that Passion will give her a second chance.

"But you should have really listened when I said you'd only get one shot!"

"I know, I know!" Jenni says.

"So, because I've been through this before," Passion says, "I know what to do."

"You do?"

"I do. I'll give you a second chance," Passion says.

"Oh, thank you so much, Passion!" Jenni screams and rushes forward for a hug. "I don't think I'll ever be able to repay you."

"I'm not concerned with that," Passion says, brushing Jenni's words away with her hands. "I want you to make the right choice this time. The right choice for *you*, that is."

"I will. I promise, and I won't let you down," Jenni says.

"Don't worry about letting me down, Jenni," Passion says, patting her heart. "Don't let *yourself* down. Go ahead and walk around again," she says, walking away.

"Thank you again!" Jenni yells as Passion disappears back inside the main office building on the lot.

She and Johnny walk toward a row of SUVs shining brightly in the afternoon sunlight.

"I do think this is the right choice considering I'll be driving it for the rest of my life. A car like this could take me anywhere," Jenni says as they walk down the row, eyeing different makes and models.

"Yes, it probably could…take you anywhere. Or *us* anywhere," Johnny says, looking away.

Jenni stops, processing what he's said.

"Probably?" she says.

"No no, I mean 'yes,'" Johnny stammers. "Yes, it will get you anywhere you need to go. It's an SUV, for goodness sake. Of course, it will get you where you need to go."

"Now, hold on," Jenni says. "What did you mean by 'probably'? Your car's great. There's no 'probably' involved," she says.

"I didn't mean that. I guess I'm nervous about you having to choose again because you made a mistake the first time. And I know your coach used to say, 'You hesitate, you die.' Right?" he says. "'Aim, point, and shoot!' Right?"

"Hey! You're supposed to be my friend!" Jenni says. She runs over to him and crosses her arms in front of him.

"I *am* your friend, but that doesn't mean I can't be nervous about your decision-making."

"Oh really?" Jenni says frustratedly.

"Yes, and I don't mean to be a jerk here, but you did rush into your first choice. You've recognized that yourself!"

"*Please*, Johnny," Jenni says sarcastically, "tell me more about my 'decision-making,'" she says in air quotes.

"You yourself know that the decision-makers in this world are the ones who make the money. That's not a coincidence. Good, bad, in-between, the people who make the decisions – especially the *tough* ones – are the ones who make the money. They get *paid* to make those decisions. So while I'm not going to lecture you about it, I do think you chose too quickly, and thank goodness Passion's understanding and forgiving enough to let you do it over again. So be the 'money maker' and make the right decision this time," Johnny says.

Jenni pauses, thinking over a potential response. She's aware that the people who love you in life often question your judgment because they don't want to see you make mistakes. They *care*. And she knows Johnny cares about her. That's without a doubt.

"You're right. Passion is something else," Jenni says. "Support me, okay? Don't judge me. I don't need you to fix me. You fix computers. You fix cars. You don't fix people," she says as she walks back over to the SUV they're standing near and peers inside.

"I'm not judging you, Jenni. And I don't want to fix you. You're not broken," he says, and they lock eyes and smile. "I want you to make the right choice."

"That's what I want too," she says.

So after Jenni decides on a new SUV – fire-engine red with three rows of seats and a luggage rack on the roof – she and Johnny head back toward the main office building on the lot. As they do, Passion sees them and walks out.

"So," Passion says, "have you decided?" She claps her hands together.

"I have! I want that red one over there," Jenni says, pointing at the nearest row.

Passion raises a hand to her head to block the sun and look into the distance.

"I see. That's a beautiful car," she says.

"It is!" Jenni says excitedly. "So can I have the keys?" she asks.

"Sure thing," Passion says. She reaches into her pocket which somehow contains the very keys Jenni needs and hands them over.

"Thank you so much!" Jenni says. She and Johnny share a smile. They make a motion to go get in the car when Passion interrupts them.

"Now, what I failed to mention is that this 'do over' doesn't come without a price."

"Oh," Jenni says, crestfallen. She looks at Johnny. "Does this mean I'll have to pay for the car?"

"No, not that kind of *price*. I meant *price* as in a task of sorts."

"A task..." Jenni says, trailing off and staring at the ground.

"Yes, and I know exactly the task. The right *price*, let's say," Passion says, trailing off. "I have a friend I want you to meet: Diego. You can take Johnny with you," Passion says.

Jenni looks up and at Johnny, who shrugs his shoulders.

"Diego's a mechanic and a businessman," Passion says, handing Jenni a slip of paper. "Here's the address. Head over there now. He's expecting you."

When Jenni and Johnny arrive at the address Passion gives them – in Jenni's new SUV, by the way – it appears to be an abandoned parking lot. There's grass growing up through the asphalt, and the streetlamps in the lot are all smashed up. There's broken glass on the ground.

"Be careful," Johnny says, as they both get out of the car.

As they do, Jenni notices a man walking toward them from far off. He waves to them, and Johnny waves back.

"Hello there!" he yells from a distance. Jenni and Johnny wait for him to get closer.

"Hi," Jenni says. "Are you Diego?" she asks.

"I am, I am," he says, coming forward to shake their hands. Diego is a short, stocky fellow who's wearing a uniform that looks like he's a had a full day of hard work. As they shake, however, Jenni notices his hands are soft and clean. His smile is warm and welcoming.

"Nice to meet you," Johnny says, smiling.

"Nice to meet you, as well. Come, come, let's sit down over here." There's a tired old picnic table to one side of the lot. It's positioned under a tree, so there's some shade.

"There, there," he says.

Jenni and Johnny sit down across from one another, and Diego sits next to Johnny.

"Nice day outside," Johnny says, making small talk. He and Jenni have no idea why they're there, or why Diego would be expecting them.

"Sure is," Diego says.

"So, Passion says you're a mechanic and a businessman? Do you work around here?" Jenni asks.

"Ah, not at the moment," Diego says.

Jenni looks at him a bit puzzled.

"Are you out of work?"

"No, no. I said I don't work around here at the moment. But in the next year or so, I'll be opening up my new shop on this here parking lot. Bought the lot yesterday." Diego is smiling from ear to ear.

"Congratulations, man!" Johnny says, shaking Diego's hand again.

"Absolutely! Congrats, Diego," Jenni says.

"Thank you, thank you. Cost me one million dollars. And that's only for the land!"

Jenni and Johnny are very impressed. For him to have bought a million-dollar lot is impressive, to say the least. She's a bit in awe of the man. Right now, the empty lot looks a mess. She can see that with some digging, however, it could become a thing of beauty one day.

"That's a lot of money!" Johnny says.

"I know, I know, but that's what it's going for these days. Great location, right off the highway. It's in an area where I know I can find good employees, so I'm very excited."

"That's great, Diego," Johnny says.

"So if you're opening a new location in a year, where's your current shop?"

"Well currently, I have three. They're all within 15 miles of here. Started with one small shop on the edge of town. It was all I could afford at the time. I've grown the business a lot over the past decade, and now I'm ready to build a flagship store. It'll be on this very spot we're sitting."

Over the next half hour, Jenni and Johnny hear Diego's story. He's the child of Mexican immigrants who moved to America before Diego was born. They helped run a small bodega in the city before moving to the suburbs and having Diego and his sister Maria. Growing up, Diego was persecuted and discriminated against because of his Mexican heritage, even though he was a legal resident of the United States. Jenni was shocked to hear about some of Diego's experiences.

However, he wouldn't let any of it get him down. He refused to feed into others' ignorant behavior, and so he made a vow to work hard, get an education, and prove his worth to everyone around him. He started with his first small mechanic's shop when he was 23 and fresh out of trade school. Now at 50, he's a year away from opening a 15,000 square-foot shop with 10 service bays and potentially upwards of 40 employees. Jenni could see how proud Diego was of himself, but it wasn't cockiness or arrogance. Not remotely.

It was humble, healthy pride.

Jenni instantly remembered her college coach teaching her about a *Ph.D.*: living life with *passion, humility,* and *discipline*. Yes, Diego has accomplished a lot, but the stores he owns aren't really the achievement. The achievement lies in doing the work itself with a *Ph.D.*

"Diego, for all that you've accomplished, you strike me as being very humble."

"I am, absolutely I am. You've got to be. At least, I don't know another way. Working hard is a reward in and of itself. I saw my first shop as a way to help people. Everyone drives a car, right? At least, around here they do. And I wanted to do something with my life that helps others. I've always been a bit of a servant leader if I do say so myself, and I saw this as an opportunity to do something I love – work with cars – and help people along the way. So I made some choices in my early 20s to put everything I had into the business, and I've been blessed with the results 10 times over. A lot of people recruit their own problems, right? Not me. I've learned to recruit as few problems as possible. I've learned to make better choices overall as the years have gone on, and it's made my life all the better," Diego says.

"Wow," Jenni says. "Tell me more about that." It was reminding her about something her college coach used to say: *elite performers never recruit their own problems*.

"Well, your ability to choose either enhances your life…or it doesn't. And I've spent the past few decades or so making the best decisions I can make in order to help others and also set up my family – really, my children – to live their own successful lives now that they're out in the world. I took my eyes off myself a long time ago and decided to look at other people instead. *That's* part of being a servant leader. Another major part is putting others before yourself and then doing the work *alongside them*," Diego says, smiling.

"That's incredible, Diego. So how many kids do you have?" Johnny asked.

Diego laughed.

"I have two, but they're not kids anymore. Alamiro is 27, and Catarina is 25. They work for me. Great kids," Diego says, smiling again.

"That's amazing. Your whole *story* is amazing," Johnny says.

"Thank you," Diego says.

"It's very clear why Passion wanted us to meet you," Jenni says.

"Oh, Passion didn't want you to meet me. She wanted *me* to meet *you*."

Jenni and Johnny look at each other.

"Huh?"

"Yep, she called me up and said that you'd made a mistake and needed to work through some stuff," he says.

"Ahhh, I see. She's not wrong," Jenni says.

"So I've got a job for you," Diego says.

Jenni looks at Johnny and grabs his hand for moral support.

"A job? As in, employment?" Jenni asks.

"Absolutely. That is, if you're up for it," Diego says.

"I think I'm up for it," Jenni says. "But we need to go over a few things. I'm not sure I'm what you're looking for. And we'd have to talk salary," she asks. She's seeing the *money* exit up ahead, and it's looking very attractive.

Diego smiles.

"Of course!" he says.

She then sends Johnny off to run an errand while Diego and Jenni walk the perimeter of the lot talking about the job. Diego makes Jenni an offer: he needs someone to manage the new location. Help get it built and off the ground. Passion has recommended her. He's willing to pay her twice what she currently makes.

"But I don't know anything about cars or mechanics," Jenni says in utter shock and disbelief.

"That's okay," Diego says. "You know how to *lead people*. *Encourage* them. *Inspire* them. At least, that's what Passion said. And she said you have a certain...spark about you. I can see it myself. And all that's more important than anything else. I'm a firm believer in hiring the right *person*, and then everything else will fall into place. Heck, I'll teach you everything you need to know about cars. Don't worry about that."

"Your kids don't want to run the new location?" Jenni asks.

"No, not really. Too much responsibility! You're about their age, so it's not really experience I'm looking for. Besides, they're both happy in the jobs they currently have. Alamiro is a mechanic at the first shop I ever opened, and Catarina does the books for two of the locations. This new one will be an entirely new ball game. I need someone fresh, someone with something to prove."

The twinkle in Jenni's eye comes back. Diego sees it, and he smiles.

"And I think I know exactly the right person," Diego says.

So in one afternoon, Jenni's life has changed.

She has traded in her hybrid for the red SUV.

She has been offered – and accepts – a new job in an unfamiliar field with a much higher salary.

She has called her boss at the nonprofit to give her two week's notice.

She takes Johnny to dinner to celebrate.

What's happening right now is that Jenni knows which exit to take – the *money* exit because working for Diego will mean a much higher salary – and she's accelerating out of that roundabout and down the exit ramp. She's made a confident choice and is looking forward to what's ahead. As confident as she is, however, only time will tell if that's the right exit for her.

JENNI'S STORY, PART TWO

So Jenni starts her new job working for Diego and helps get the flagship store built and operational, and she loves it. She's really good at it, in fact. Diego was right: he taught her everything she needs to know about cars (which wasn't much, after all), and the rest very much did fall into place. She really loves the people who work for Diego, and they've had her respect from the very first day of her employment. She's also making twice as much as she made at her last job, and that part's been a little overwhelming for her. She's not even thirty, and she's making six figures. She almost doesn't know what to do with it all every time her paycheck hits her bank account.

In somewhat of a predictable move, our girl Jenni starts to get a little full of herself after about a year or so of having worked for Diego. She's so good at her job at the new location that Diego's recently had her traveling to and from his other shops to keep an eye on things there too. She's worked hard to manage so many people, and she thinks one day that it's time to really reward herself.

In other words, she sees that shiny exit up ahead while she's in the roundabout of her job – the *perceived success* exit – and thinks that it's the exit for her.

She calls Johnny one night after hours of thinking.

"I'm ready to get a different car!" she says.

"You're kidding," Johnny says, deadpan.

"No, I'm not. And I'll either have your support, or I won't," Jenni says.

"Well, can I at least ask what's brought on this change of heart? Again?"

"Johnny, the second I feel like you're judging me..." she says.

"I'm not judging you, Jenni. I'm shocked you want to go back and do this again. It's not like you," he says.

"Well, apparently, it *is* me. It's my decision. I've been working really hard, and I think I want a fancier car. Or maybe a *second* car. I don't know! I think I deserve this!" Jenni says.

No sooner does she say that then she finds herself back on the car lot. Johnny is going to sit this one out because he's got a big project to complete for work, and he trusts that Passion will help Jenni resolve the situation once and for all.

As Jenni arrives at the lot, Passion sees her and immediately rushes over.

"Back again? What has it been, a little over a year?" Passion asks.

"Yes, about that long. I'm a little shocked to be back, myself. It's a little embarrassing, to be honest," Jenni says.

Passion takes her arm gently, and they start walking down a row of cars.

"Don't be embarrassed, my dear. We've all been there. We've all made decisions that in hindsight, we should have made differently. But what we have to do is get to the bottom of why you want to make another change," Passion says.

"Absolutely. Well, the thing is, I've been working for Diego for about a year now. He's great, by the way. And I work really hard," Jenni says.

"I bet you do. A lot of us do," Passion says.

"I know, but I'm in a position where I make a lot more money, and I think I'd like to drive something fancier than what I've got right now."

Passion stops walking and turns to look Jenni in the eye.

"Fancier? Why, so people can look at you?"

"No, no, that's not it. I don't know, I've never had a really nice car."

"I hate to tell you, Jenni, but that SUV I've given you *is* really nice. And I thought you wanted a bigger vehicle to accommodate a family down the road," Passion says as they start walking again.

"I know. I'm sorry. That came out wrong. It *is* a nice car. Of course, it is. I was thinking that while I'm still young and have nothing tying me down, why not drive a car that's a bit frivolous and doesn't make practical sense?"

"Jenni, I'm going to be honest. This doesn't really sound like you," Passion says.

"Johnny said the same thing! But I'm telling you, this is me. I'm the one making the decision. And I'm prepared to pay for it this time..."

"No, no. That's not part of the deal. I'm supposed to be giving you a car for you to drive for the rest of your life. I'm not abandoning that notion simply because we've had a few hiccups here and there. But I have to tell you...I don't really like the sound of it."

They continue walking in silence for a bit.

94

"What makes you think that, Passion? I respect your opinion, and I want to know what you think," Jenni says.

"Well, I'm proud of you for the work you're doing for Diego. But I don't want you to lose sight of what's important. And yes, cars are important. Heck, I've made them my life's work. But I think the SUV you've got right now is more than enough car for you, and honestly, I'm at a little bit of a loss in comprehending why you want to make another change."

They've come to a stopping point beneath the biggest tree on the car lot. Even though there's a lot of people on the lot again today, all the noise and chatter are drowned out from their current spot. The importance of the moment is not lost on either woman.

"I know. I know it may look strange from the outside. But trust me on this. I know it's what I want to do."

Passion sighs and looks off into the distance.

"I certainly hope you're right," she says.

So Jenni convinces Passion to go along with the new change.

Against the advice from those around her, Jenni has taken the *perceived success* exit because she wants other people to notice her and her success, even if she doesn't want to admit it.

There's a bit of a back and forth with Passion about the new car. But in the end, Jenni walks away with a car she's dreamed of ever since her uncle had one when she was younger: a black Ferrari 812 GTS. It seats two and is an absolutely absurd choice, but it's fun and flashy and Jenni is caught up in the moment.

Also remember, even though she makes quite a bit of money working for Diego, Passion is still voluntarily on the hook for giving Jenni the car. No money involved. This is Passion backing up her initial claim of wanting to give Jenni a car because of that spark, that special quality she caught in Jenni's eye from across the crowded car lot on that first day they met. That special something that sets Jenni apart from her peers. From everyone else, really.

So Jenni has rewarded herself for a job well done and drives home in her Ferrari with a big smile on her face. She catches a man's eye at a stoplight and smiles at him, thinking, *I've made it.*

Jenni's phone rings one night after she's gotten home from work; she's worked out and showered and is relaxing on the couch when it rings. She checks her phone.

It's Johnny.

"Hello?" she says, thinking to herself, *I haven't talked to him in weeks…*

"Hey, Jenni," Johnny says. He sounds upset, like something's wrong.

"How are you? Are you okay?" she asks, sitting up. She checks her watch. 9:45 P.M.

"Uh, actually, I'm not."

"You're not," Jenni says.

"No, I'm not. I need to talk."

"We're talking now," she says.

"I mean in person. I need to see you and for us to talk in person."

"Okay, how soon? It's almost 10."

"Tonight. It needs to be tonight. Can I come over?"

"Sure," she says. And 15 minutes later, Johnny is sitting on the couch in Jenni's apartment.

"Can I get you something to drink?" she asks, puttering nervously around in the kitchen. She's nervous. She hasn't seen him in a few weeks, and it's late, and she has no idea what's so pressing that it couldn't have waited until tomorrow.

"No, I'm good. Come sit," he says, patting the couch next to him.

She moves into the living room from the kitchen and turns on a lamp. She sits down next to him and smiles nervously.

"Are you okay?" she asks.

"I'm not. But that's what I want to talk about."

"Okay, sure. I know we haven't seen each other in weeks..."

"Months, Jenni. It's been three months."

"Three months?" Jenni asks, looking off.

"Yes, three months. Remember? We'd made plans for lunch one day and I texted you ahead of time, but you never showed up. You stood me up." He's not mad when he says this. He's disappointed, which is worse.

"I did?"

"Yes! You did!" He starts to get upset as she fails to remember this moment. "We said we'd meet for lunch at El Agave, but you never showed. This would have been in May."

"May..." Jenni says. "May was a busy month."

"May, June, July. They all seem busy to you."

"Hey, I have a lot on my plate. I'm doing so much more for Diego than I ever thought I'd be doing."

"I'm aware."

"And I like it! The money's great, and I love working with the people I work with."

"Are any of them your friends?"

"Friends?"

"Yeah, friends. Do you see any of them outside of work?"

Jenni has to think for a moment.

"No, I guess I don't."

"I bet you don't," Johnny says self-righteously.

"So what? I forgot about lunch that day and you decide not to call me for three months?" She's gotten up from the couch by now and stands away from him, leaning against the column that separates the living room and kitchen. It's dark in the apartment, but they can still see each other.

"You didn't call me either! It's a two-way street!" Johnny says emphatically. "And after you got that Ferrari...my goodness."

"I knew it," Jenni says. "I knew you hated that car. You're jealous. You're holding me back!"

"Holding you back? And no, I don't hate it! It's simply not...you. Or maybe it is. I don't even know anymore."

"What if it is me? What if I really like it?" Jenni says.

"I think you do like it, but I think you like what it represents instead of liking the car itself."

That stops Jenni in her tracks. There's silence as they both gauge what's been said.

"So this is what you wanted to talk about with me at 10 PM on a Tuesday? How much you hate my car?" Jenni asks.

"Oh, stop. And no, it's not. Well, partly, yes. In a way, it's like *you* became that car. Or the car became you. I don't know. But there's a lot more."

"Really," Jenni says.

"Yes, please come sit back down."

After thinking about it for a second, Jenni slowly walks back to the couch to take a seat, this time a bit further away from him.

"I got a job offer," Johnny says.

"That's great!" Jenni says, genuinely excited for him.

"In California," he says.

Jenni sits back, deflated.

"California?" she says. "California?"

"Yes, California. San Francisco to be exact. My company is opening a new branch, and they want me to lead the team they're sending out to get it going."

"Wow," Jenni says. She's sitting back in the cushions, hands folded in her lap. "I mean, that's such a great opportunity."

"It is," Johnny says.

"But it's so far!" Jenni says. She won't look at Johnny now.

"I know. It is far. That's what I wanted to talk about."

"Well, you're going to take it, right?"

"I haven't accepted the position yet, no."

"Why not?"

"Because I wanted to talk to you about it."

"I appreciate that. I do. But it sounds like it's too good an opportunity to turn down."

"Well, I can certainly see both sides of it. Sure. New city, new way of life. New salary," he says.

"Right," she says.

"But I don't think I want to go unless..."

"Unless?" Jenni truly has no idea what he's about to say.

"Unless you come with me."

"Me?!"

"Yes, you! You can say we're friends all you want, and yes, we definitely started as friends all those years ago. But I know what I know. And you've always been the one."

He's reached forward to take her hand, so she's looking at him when she says this.

"I don't know what to say," she says. This is all happening really fast, and her thoughts are a jumble in her head. Johnny's priorities are shifting, some of which might include her in a major way. But she's got priorities of her own, obviously.

"Why me?!" she says.

"I think I'm falling in love with you, Jenni," he says.

Jenni's jaw hits the floor, and the lights go out.

Amid the temporary blackout in her apartment, Johnny has given Jenni a lot to think about, obviously. They light some candles and place them around the living room and proceed to talk about their feelings for one another.

Johnny says that ever since that day when Jenni said "our kids" in front of Passion that he's been thinking. *She's my best friend. Why shouldn't she be my partner, my teammate?*

Jenni admits that she's had feelings for him for a long time, as well, but didn't really know what to do about it considering she was working so hard for Diego and pushing her personal life to the back burner. She's put her career first to complete her checklist toward success. She still doesn't know what to do. Simply because he's professed his love for her doesn't mean she's going to fall into his arms and say goodbye to the life she's worked so hard to construct for herself.

They talk for hours. The conversation doesn't come to a resolution, but they decide together that Johnny's got to take the job offer in California and that they'll continue to talk and see where things go. Jenni's simply not ready to leave the opportunities she's made for herself in working for Diego – she loves the work *and* the money *and* the perceived success – and she wants to see how it all plays out.

Johnny understands.

He's a little hurt that she's not ready to throw caution to wind and go with him, but he respects her choice. That's the beauty of free will, but in most cases, there are consequences. And hurt feelings.

He leaves the apartment at 4 AM and is dog tired at work the next day. Jenni's up at 6 as usual, ready to attack the day.

What Jenni fails to see, and what a lot of us so often fail to see, is that our ego gets in the way of so much of our decision-making. We get our feet under us a little and often think very highly of ourselves, whether it's because of our job, an award, an accomplishment, or a good grade on an exam, for example. We start to think, *Well, I'm simply the best. I'm awesome. I'm invincible.*

We see that *perceived success* exit coming around the bend and think, *that's the exit for me.*

A certain amount of self-confidence is healthy, but being full of oneself is never the way to go. Perceived success is an illusion, and it's only comforting when people actually view you as successful. But how often do people not do and say the things we want them to do and say?

Depending on other people's views and opinions in order to feel successful is a recipe for disaster, plain and simple.

Times moves on, and Jenni spends the next several weeks ignoring her feelings and forgetting about her conversation with Johnny. She compartmentalizes her feelings by coping with work and other distractions. She doesn't recognize it at first, but she's in a state of *dis-ease*: that state in which we have a pit in our stomachs and know something isn't right.

I'm not talking about stress. *Dis-ease* is something different.

It's when you're uneasy about things and may or may not know why.

In Jenni's case, after their conversation the night of the blackout, she's expecting that they'll go their separate ways for a bit and then talk again as soon as they get some things figured out on their own respective ends. However, over the course of the next week or so, Jenni's back to thinking mostly about herself. She's not thinking about Johnny because whenever she does, she starts to feel like something's off. She'd rather ignore those feelings and live in the moment. She's driving that Ferrari and living her best life; at least in *her* opinion, she is. Johnny has moved to California by that time, and he may as well be on the moon for as close as California feels to her.

On a seemingly regular Wednesday afternoon, Diego stops by the flagship store and pops his head into Jenni's office.

"Jenni!" he says.

"Diego! Come in!" she says, getting up from her desk to welcome him into her office.

"Thank you, thank you," he says. He's in his everyday uniform from working in the shop. "I don't want to get your chair dirty," he says as he moves in front of one of the club chairs in Jenni's office.

"Don't worry about that whatsoever. Take a load off, my friend," she says, holding her hand out for him to take a seat.

"Thank you," he says, sighing as he plops into the chair. It's toward the end of the day, and he's recently finished a long shift.

"So what brings you by today?" Jenni asks.

"Well, an idea popped into my head this morning, and I wanted to run it by you," Diego says.

"About the company?"

"No," Diego says. "About you."

"Oh really?" Jenni asks.

"Yes, really. I'd like to set you up on a date with my son, Alamiro," Diego says smiling.

Jenni has worked with Alamiro for essentially as long as she's worked for Diego. She sees him all the time at the Branch Avenue shop because he's a mechanic there, and a really good one at that. He's a nice guy, that's for sure.

But a date?

"Wow, that's...interesting," Jenni says.

She's attempting to strike a balance between being kind about it – Diego is her boss, after all – while not committing to the idea yet. Oddly enough, an image of Johnny pops into her mind, and she does her best to expel it immediately. Now was not the time to think about Johnny and whatever they...are.

"He's a wonderful young man, Jenni. I mean, you already know that because you work with him. But he's getting to that age where his mother and I would like to see him settle down. She mentioned your name the other night at dinner, and I've been tossing the idea around ever since," Diego says.

Jenni isn't crazy about them tossing her name around like she's some sort of commodity, but in a way, it's also flattering for them to think of her.

"I see," Jenni says, thinking and looking down at the floor.

"Would you be open to it?" Diego asks.

He's sitting on the edge of his seat looking like an eager child in school. In this moment, Jenni does not want to hurt his feelings, nor does she want to jeopardize her job or have Diego change the way he thinks of her. She knows she's got to tread lightly in this situation.

In other words, she sees the *distractions* exit coming up around the bend, and she knows full well that she should not take the exit. She's never looked at Alamiro that way, and she's still exploring the nature of her feelings for Johnny. Whether she needs to pause her career to pursue him and potentially build a family, or can she do both?

That state of *dis-ease* rears its ugly head again in this moment.

She needs more time to think about it, but she doesn't want to keep Diego waiting.

"Sure. Why not?" Jenni says, smiling and holding her arms up in a shrug.

"Excellent! I'll give him your number, and you can expect a call from him soon!" Diego says, and before she knows it, he's gone.

It's about a week later when she finds herself sitting across from Diego's son Alamiro at a fancy restaurant on the south side of town. They're at a little French bistro near the water.

Alamiro was on time picking her up, he's dressed as neat as a pin, and he's had a huge smile on his face the entire time they've been together. The drive over was great; they were chatting the entire time, and he was a responsible driver the whole way. He opened Jenni's door as she got in and out of the car, and he opened the door for her when they went into the restaurant. Initially, Jenni had said yes to the date because she wanted to please Diego while also distracting herself from thinking about Johnny. So far, so good.

"So," Alamiro says as they're chatting over their first glass of wine, "how do you like working for my dad?" He's still smiling, and it's hard not to be in a good mood around him.

"It's great! Ever since the day we met, I knew he was a good person. It was out of this world. And I've learned so much from him already," Jenni says as she sips her wine.

"That's awesome. He says you're wonderful at your job, but I already knew that," Alamiro says. There's a twinkle in his eye that makes him look like he's out of a movie.

"You're nice to say that," Jenni says.

"It's true! Everyone's been blown away with your leadership and kindness. The results you've achieved around here. You've made quite an impression on everyone," he says.

"Thank you for saying that. I'm lucky to have the job I have," Jenni says.

"So what initially brought you to the area, though? Dad said you were working for a non-profit when he hired you," Alamiro says.

"That's right, I was. I'd been in grad school in D.C. and then found the job at the non-profit and was looking to move. I was excited! It was purposeful work; I didn't choose it for the money. And we played some away games here when I was in college, so I've always liked this place," Jenni says.

"Nice," Alamiro says. "You played college basketball, right?"

"Yes, I did."

"How was that?"

"To be honest, it was intense. Looking back, I almost don't know how I did it. It was Division 1, and it was basically like having a full-time job on top of having the full-time job of going to school. But I had a great coach and wonderful teammates, so overall, it was a positive experience."

"You liked your coach?" Alamiro asks.

"I most certainly did. I know a lot of college coaches get a bad rap for having high expectations and demanding excellence, but my coach managed to do all that while simultaneously loving us fiercely. And we knew that. We knew she cared about us. So we'd go out there on the  court and fight like crazy and play together, and we won a ton of games doing so," Jenni says, staring off into the distance.

"You've got me missing it!" she says, looking back at Alamiro.

"That sounds amazing, actually. And yes, I know some people who look back on their college playing career, and they don't have a lot of fond memories. I'm happy for you that your experience was really different," Alamiro says.

"It was. I suppose I was lucky. And I was a darn good basketball player," she says.

"I heard that, as well! Living up to your nickname!"

"Exactly," Jenni says, sipping her wine. "So what about you? How do you like working for your dad? Off the record, of course," she says, laughing softly.

"Oh, I love it," he says. "I really do. I know a lot of people say that mixing business with family is a recipe for disaster, but we don't see it that way. And I think that's because he set the tone immediately – as in, when I was hired at 16 to sweep the floors and clean the bathrooms – that when I was at work, he wasn't my dad. He was my boss. And I internalized that and have never looked back. I think he goes a little easier on my sister, but that's because she's the baby of the family!" Alamiro says with a laugh.

"See, that's another reason why I like Diego so much. He's so fair. I've honestly never heard an employee utter a negative word about him," Jenni says.

"Yep, he's pretty great."

"So you've worked for him since you were 16?"

"Yep, a little over a decade now, I guess. Wow," he says.

"So cool. I'm sure you feel like that time has flown," Jenni says.

"I do. I really do. But I feel like I'm doing meaningful work that gets *results*, and I'm surrounded by people I love," he says.

"You're pretty lucky too, then," Jenni says.

"I suppose I am," he says.

Their dinner arrives, and they continue chatting throughout the meal. On the surface, it would appear that he and Jenni are hitting it off. Yet whenever there's even a minor lull in the conversation as they eat, Jenni finds herself thinking about Johnny. The initial shimmer and shine of the date eventually wear off, and she's left with so many questions.

How's California going?

What's Johnny doing right now?

Is he thinking about me?

Does he miss me?

It's only once the check has arrived late in the evening – sun having set long ago behind the mountains in the distance – does Jenni realize that this is all wrong. She recognizes this feeling for what it is: a sense of dis-ease.

Johnny, on the other hand, puts her at a state of *ease*. And while being in that state isn't necessarily easy – especially when you have to decipher lots of feelings and emotions – it means you're at ease and in a relaxed state, and this is where the magic happens.

When she thinks of Johnny now, she feels happy and content and excited. As she sits there across from Alamiro, she realizes a few things.

She shouldn't have said yes in order to please Diego.

She shouldn't have gone on the date as a way of distracting herself from her feelings for Johnny.

She shouldn't have put Alamiro – a perfectly nice young man – through an evening that she knew on some level would never go anywhere in the long run. He would have been a placeholder until she'd figured things out about Johnny, her soulmate and teammate for life.

Her stomach is in knots. She reaches to pay for the bill, but he tries to stop her.

"What are you doing?" he asks.

"No really, I need to pay for this," she says.

"You do not need to pay for any of this," he says.

"I do," she says, taking the check. She lays her credit card in the plastic tray and sets it on the end of the table. She sits back in her chair and sighs.

"What is it?" Alamiro asks.

"I'm so sorry, Alamiro. This was a mistake," she says.

"A mistake?" He is so hurt in this moment that Jenni almost wishes she'd never said anything.

"Yes, a mistake. I mean, you're basically perfect, and any other person would be so lucky to go on a date with you. But I'm not that person," she says.

He looks utterly devastated.

"I'm not sure I understand. Is it something I said? I thought the night was going great," he says, leaning forward and folding his hands in front of him on the table.

"It's not anything you said, I promise. I have feelings for someone else, to be honest. And I thought I could tamp all that down and ignore those feelings, but sitting here with you and knowing I should have butterflies and all that because you're great…has been eye-opening. I can see now that my stomach only flips upside down for one person," she says.

"I see," he says, sitting back in his seat. "Can I ask who that person is?" he asks.

"His name's Johnny. Your dad's actually met him. He's someone I've known since college, and I thought we were only ever supposed to be friends. But the past few months being apart from him – he lives in California now – have been the weirdest few months of my life. I've been running away from him for awhile now. I'm ready to run *to* him," she says. "I can't believe I'm saying all this to you. It's obnoxious," she says.

"No, it's actually not. I mean, I'm upset because I really like you, and it would be awesome to see where things could go. But if you're in love with someone else, then you've got to pursue that. Shoot your shot! You have to," he says.

Jenni can't believe he's being supportive of her in this moment. But as Diego's son, it makes perfect sense. They're good, *selfless* people.

"Thank you, Alamiro," Jenni says. "I don't know what to say."

"You don't have to say anything else. I appreciate your honesty," he says. He smiles at her. "I'm okay, really," he says.

Later on, after he's dropped her back off at home and they've said goodbye, Jenni realizes she's left her house key in her car. She gets into the Ferrari in her dress and sits in the driver's seat. She starts moving things around in the console to look for the key when she notices that the seatbelt has chafed her arm.

"Ow!" she says, rubbing a spot on her elbow. "That hurt," she says.

She finds the key and sits back in the seat, having moved the rough seatbelt out of the way. In that moment, she has gained the ability to *recognize* how wrong the date actually was. How wrong this *car* is, for goodness sake. How wrong all of it is. How wrong it is because the one thing she's needed her whole life – the person who's been in front of her the entire time – is the thing she's been running from for months.

She's been in a state of dis-ease for awhile now, and she's been miserable. Being in a state of dis-ease, by the way, will put you in a state of *actual disease* if you remain in this state for the duration. Jenni's heard stories about this: people who live in misery and eventually acquire some sort of life-altering disease or condition.

Jenni knows she's making the right move now that could potentially save her own life.

And while she took the *distractions* exit because she thought it was the right choice at the time, she now sees how wrong that was, as well. She didn't need a distraction. She needed focused intensity on her relationship with Johnny but fell into the trap of being distracted by people pleasing.

She vows to make it right and gets out of the car with a smile and a newfound purpose.

DYING TO YOUR OWN EGO

So as we see Jenni come to a major realization, let's stop for a moment.

I want to take some time to talk about one other very important concept that I've learned in my life, something I want you to learn, as well. Something that Jenni is learning and experiencing as we speak.

In my life, I've found that when I get a bit too big for my britches, things always have a way of coming back down to reality. Sometimes, it's in a subtle way. But sometimes, we get into a spot when we end up completely veering off the path we've chosen. We're metaphorically driving our car, and then depending on what's happening and what our mindset may or may not be, we start to drift away from the road. But you know how some roads have rumble strips outside the white lines to wake up sleepy drivers?

In our lives, when we run that car off the road, we've got to do our absolute best to steer it back between the white lines. And often with me, God has a way of making me see the error of my ways. And the root of many of my problems in the past has been my own pride. My own ego.

I'm sure there are many times when you yourself have gotten caught up in your own pride and ego. And whether it's God or the universe or whatever you want to call it, when that car starts to veer off the road and the rumble strips start screaming, you need to pay attention and keep it within the white lines!

That's what's happening to Jenni at the moment.

She's worked for Diego for a good while and has truly made an impact on his business. From being initially hired to manage one location to now managing all of his locations, Jenni has a lot on her plate and has been doing a great job. She's earning her paycheck 10 times over. She's thinking highly of herself, and who could blame her? A female in a predominantly male industry, and she's in charge of day-to-day operations, essentially. It's a big deal.

But what has she lost in this process?

What she didn't tell Johnny in their late-night conversation on the couch in her apartment is that she hadn't spoken to her parents in several weeks and that she had to cancel her annual trip to Cherry Grove with her only sister, Cameron. She didn't want to tell Johnny that other important relationships in her life were hurting because it would have only reinforced his point, and she wasn't ready to do that. She wasn't ready for him to be right, once again.

The trip she canceled with Cameron was the trip they've made together every year since college, but she had to bail this year because she simply couldn't find the time to take off work. The flagship branch was doing a sales promotion that same weekend as the trip, and she simply couldn't *not* be there.

As you can imagine, Cameron was less than thrilled that Jenni canceled on her. Cameron still went on the trip. She took a friend from work, but it wasn't the same. She wanted that time with Jenni.

So another year would have to go by before they could plan that trip again.

How many of us have been guilty of doing something like that?

I'm talking about times when we have had to alter or cancel plans altogether with family or friends because of a work obligation. Now sometimes, this is truly unavoidable. I don't think anyone's family or friends would want you to take vacation days at the threat of truly getting behind or losing your job. However, I think a lot of us have been in a spot where we could take a few vacation days to spend time with family or friends, and instead, we shrug it off and stay at work.

I tell you what: none of us are getting any younger, right? You're as young as you'll ever be as you read this sentence right now.

Cancelling plans is something we've all done, but think about what's lost when we do that. No day is ever guaranteed, but Jenni's been living like every day and the next are fully guaranteed for as long as she wants.

And one major thing she's losing in the shuffle is her relationship with Johnny. When she tells him that night on the couch that she's had feelings for him for awhile, she means it. It was no accident when she said "our kids" that day with him in front of Passion. She said it because subconsciously (and consciously, to be honest) she's thought about starting a family with Johnny. Every time she allows herself a moment to slow down, take her eyes off herself, and feel something, it's Johnny she sees. She can only visualize life *with him*.

This is a man she's known since college, and she's always been able to be herself around him. He's never judged her for anything. He's never tried to get her to become someone or something she's not; he's never rejected her. He's never laughed at her. He's been fiercely loyal and has accepted her for who she is. He challenges her from time to time, sure, but any good friend should do that. It's been that way for as long as they've known each other, and honestly, it's always been the most attractive thing about him. She loves him because he lets her be herself, unapologetically.

And yet, during these months and years she's worked for Diego, nothing else has really mattered other than her job and advancing her career.  She's taken Johnny for granted, thinking that no matter when she calls or shows up, he'll still be ready and waiting. That's why the late-night conversation caught her so off guard: she couldn't believe that he was even slightly prepared to move away and live a life separate from her. There's no logical reason why she should think he would have stuck around forever waiting for her, but she still thought, in a way, that that's how it was going to go.

And now…California.

She wanted him to take it because it's a great opportunity, but she also wanted him to stay with her because she's…well, because she's Jenni. She's a catch. She's *his* catch. And she's met her match. On some level, they've both always known this.

But there he was, ready to move away. And without her. For another life.

Jenni wonders where things went wrong.

Had their timing been off? And if so, why?

Because healthy and fulfilling relationships *are* often about timing: both good and bad. Relationships are often successful because the timing is great: people are on the same page, they're at the same stage in life, they're able to reciprocate "I love you" to one another. And relationships often fail because the timing is wrong: people are on completely different pages, at different stages in their respective lives, and one's feelings may be ahead of the other's.

Jenni feels that she's ready to get this figured out with Johnny once and for all. If it's been about timing, then she's ready to make the changes she needs to make to get it right.

With that said, this final important concept I want to discuss with you is this:

> **You must die to your own ego to find true contentment.**

Jenni needs to die to her own ego before she can find contentment.

She's been way too caught up in her job and her accomplishments. In a way, I can't blame her because it's easy to let success go to your head. At least, I've found it to be easy. Winning at the D1 level – and all the privileges and niceties it comes with – was easy to get wrapped up in, like

I've said. That job was *my* Ferrari. I often let my pride and ego get in the way. Jenni rewarded herself with that car because of the hard work she was putting in for Diego, and in a way, she *should* celebrate her hard work and success. That's not what I'm saying at all. I'm not saying we shouldn't celebrate our successes, our wins. Of course, those things should be celebrated.

What we shouldn't do, however, is celebrate those things in terms of letting our ego muddy up the things that actually matter in life: *people*, relationships, our mental and physical well-being. And Jenni's done exactly that.

The "Ferrari" mentality took over at some point, and she lost sight of some very important things.

And then, when Johnny sits her down on the couch and starts talking about those things and confronting her with the reality of certain choices she's made, she hears him but doesn't yet have the humility to process or act on what he's saying.

When Jenni is on the couch that night listening to Johnny talk about his feelings and the way he sees things and whatnot, she hears him. She does. But she's not able to absorb things in the moment. What he's told her would take anyone time to absorb, so in a way, she *should* take her time. What he's saying is so important. It shouldn't be a one-and-done conversation. But she simply couldn't wrap her head around it at the time.

How would it work? How would they make the distance *work?*

Her career was a sure bet, but a relationship could get scary and uncertain.

Along with dealing with these questions that she had no answers for, she then tried to distract herself and ignore her feelings for him.

So rather than take the *distractions* exit, this was a time when Jenni – and when we, in certain moments – needed to *accelerate* into our next move, committing to the next stop with confidence. Jenni's simply been in another roundabout: the complacency she's felt from the success she's had working for Diego.

But now's the moment when she needs to recognize that her rightful exit is coming up: the *relationships* exit. The opportunity has come along for her to pursue her feelings for Johnny, feelings that are reciprocated. And while she made a mistake by going on a date with Alamiro and people-pleasing with Diego, she can make things right. She can accelerate out of that roundabout and take the *relationships* exit to pursue Johnny and what a relationship with him might mean for her. For *them* as a couple.

As a basketball coach, I sometimes talk about the G.A.S. concept, which means "get a stop." Jenni's not playing defense here, but she needs to give it some *gas* and take that exit! She's not nicknamed One-Shot for no good reason. The opportunity has presented itself to her, and she's got to take it. She has to summon the courage and confidence to take the risk and shoot her shot.

But in doing so, Jenni will need to learn in the coming weeks and months – and often, it can take even longer – that she will have to die to her own ego in order to take this next step with Johnny and have it really mean something. She needs to learn to celebrate her successes while not letting them cloud her perspective on the things in life that are most important. She needs to see that while working for Diego has been very fulfilling, no job on Earth ever loves you back. She's got someone standing in front of her literally saying "I'm falling in love with you," and she needs to recognize that moments like this don't come along too often in life. And no job is worth passing up a chance at true love. No way, no how.

If Jenni is going to take this chance and die to her own ego, doing so will require a lot of self-reflection and a search for relevancy, things that many of us are often unwilling to do. Looking in the mirror can be incredibly difficult to do, especially so on a consistent basis. But I'm telling you, the more you do this with yourself – and on a regular basis – the more perspective you can offer to your own world and whatever it is you're going through. I could argue that because Jenni *hasn't* been doing this, she's gotten herself into the predicament she's in. She's been too focused on the *things* in life and not on the people.

And Johnny's prepared to move on because of it.

So Jenni has to die to her own ego to create a "we" with Johnny in order to set herself up for real happiness. Not something shallow that will be gone before she knows it. But a real, lasting happiness with Johnny. She's learned that she doesn't need another person in order to feel fulfilled, but that the idea of being with Johnny feels right and good and true. And why would she stay on the East Coast in a job that can replace her, as any job can obviously replace any one of us, instead of pursuing the one true love of her life?

Once she sat down to really think about it, it actually wasn't that hard of a decision. Jenni had been living like every tomorrow was promised to her, when in reality, it's not promised to any of us. She was tired of running through every *what if* her brain could come up.

She's also learned not to run from certain things in life. Instead, she's running *toward* things. *People*, really. Like she says to Alamiro that night at dinner, she wants to run *to* Johnny. She wants to do this instead of running away from the risks of having her heart broken or from the risks of not being able to find a new job in a new city that's completely foreign to her. Doing what she's doing is risky as all get-out, but she's willing to do it.

Jenni wants to be great at whatever she does – a friend, an employee, a partner, a wife – and doing so requires a lot of focused intensity and time. And being risk-averse can prevent many of us from ever taking that leap of faith that life often requires. The reward – a resounding contentment and fulfillment – is worth it.

And that's what I want people to take away from this book.

This book is a love story in a lot of ways.

Yes, it's a book about elite performance and yielding in and out of life's roundabouts and choosing the right exits. It's about *all* those things. But above all, it's a love story. It's about making tough decisions, jumping two feet in, and making those bold choices that come to define our entire life.

In Jenni's case, she has stopped worrying about *things* and has started focusing on people. She's learned to embrace the present moment with people who have her best interests in mind – in this case especially, that's Johnny – and she can't wait around until the stars are perfectly aligned for her to make a move. If we all sat around waiting for the perfect moment to take this risk or that risk, we'd be sitting around forever.

There is never going to be a perfect moment.

There's only the here and now.

And while the prettier things in life are simply that – *pretty* – they remain things. A Ferrari is very nice, but does it mean its driver is *better* than the person next to them at the stop sign? Not necessarily. People should not be defined by the things they possess, cars included. We live in a world that places way too much value in those things. If you want to drive a nice car and can afford to do so, have at it. But don't let that car define you.

Because as many of us know with life, things come and go. *Cars* come and go. People also come and go, and that's why we need to hang on to those who mean the world to us. Because ultimately, not much else matters.

Build your life on a foundation of brick (the people you love) and not sand (things).

Life is a love story, after all.

JENNI'S STORY,
PART THREE

A month has passed since Jenni's date with Alamiro, and Johnny's been in California for a couple of months.

He's spent that time getting settled and becoming accustomed to his new job. It's very demanding, but he's biking almost every evening to help release some stress and stay in shape. Mostly when he's on those bike rides, he's thinking of Jenni.

They've talked every day.

Jenni is still very busy with work, but she's shifted her thinking to focus on the *people* in her life. The people who matter most. Her parents. Her sister Cameron. Johnny.

And while focusing on those relationships, it's confirmed to her that her job working for Diego is only a job. It's not her purpose on Earth. She's learning to see that while she is really good  at her job, it is not part of her DNA. At the end of the day, she's simply *Jenni*.

During a conversation one night on the phone a few weeks ago, Jenni told Johnny of a powerful moment she'd had with Diego recently. She'd been speaking with Diego about potentially taking two weeks off to go to the beach with her sister Cameron. This was the trip she'd canceled the summer before, but she wasn't prepared to do that two consecutive times. So she'd approached Diego about taking the last two weeks of June off. The conversation went something like this:

"So yeah, it'd be great if I could take those two weeks off to go to Cherry Grove, but I understand if you'd rather I not."

"Go, Jenni. Of course! Go," Diego had said. He made a "shooing" motion with his hands as further encouragement of him wanting her to go.

"Wait...go?

"Yes! Of course, go. You haven't asked for that amount of time off in all the time you've worked for me. Of course, I want you to go."

"But I thought-"

"What? That I'd say *no*?" He was almost laughing.

"Yes! I thought you'd say no."

He looked hurt.

"Jenni! Why would you think that?" he asked, his hands over his heart melodramatically.

"Because it's a long time to ask off for, and I have so many day-to-day responsibilities. I thought it'd be too hard for you to manage while I was gone."

He started laughing.

"Jenni, listen to yourself. I started this business myself in a tiny garage a decade ago, and now I own five shops. You are incredible, and I love having you on the team. But that's it. We're a *team*. The walls won't cave in if you take a two-week vacation."

Jenni was floored.

"Now go, scoot. Go make your plans and have a wonderful vacation."

Diego stood up to walk her out of the office and hugged her on her way out. Jenni had walked to the car in a full stupor.

She often thought of herself as the glue that held the business together, but in that moment, she realized that in fact, *Diego* was the glue. She felt silly for thinking otherwise. She cried in the car on the way home.

In retelling this conversation to Johnny, she'd gotten choked up on the phone.

"But don't you see what he was really saying?" Johnny said. "His operation is so big that it will keep going even without you. Like, you're a great employee and all, but life will go on without you."

And Jenni had cried some more. Think about it: the job she'd put her blood, sweat, and tears into for years didn't really need her at the end of the day. While those weren't Diego's exact words, that's basically what he was saying. And it was very hard for her to hear.

So one afternoon, Jenni calls Johnny on a Saturday. She knows he's home because they'd talked the night before and he had nothing going on the next day. She wants to catch him at a time when he's free.

"Hey, my dear," Johnny says as he answered the phone.

"Hi, buddy," she says.

"What are you up to? What is it, noon there?"

"Yep, noon. Going for a walk. Tracy's out of town, and I'm watching her dog. Gotta go check on him." Tracy is a mutual friend of theirs from college.

"Gotcha. Well, that's nice of you."

"It is, haha," Jenni says.

"Very funny. Such a humanitarian," Johnny says jokingly.

"Hey now, I'm a nice lady," Jenni says, laughing.

"I never said you weren't!" he says.

"I know, I know," she says. "So hey, listen, I've been thinking a lot."

"Oh goodness," he says. "Jenni's been thinking!"

"Oh, stop. I've been thinking. A lot. And I've been thinking about you. A lot," she says.

Jenni can almost hear Johnny smile through the phone.

"Oh really," he says.

"Really, I have been. And I know we've argued and fought and all that stuff all rolled up together, but I've really learned some things over the past few months. You being away actually helped."

"Gee, thanks," he says.

"No, no, stop. You know what I mean. It cleared my head a bit. Actually, not a bit. It cleared my head a lot. Diego helped too," she says.

"Good, I'm glad to hear it," he says. "So have you come to any conclusions?" he asks.

"I have. Quite a few actually," she says.

"Do tell," he says, sitting up on the couch.

"Well, I've decided that I don't need a job to feel content or accomplished. I know that feeling content comes from other things. Loving myself. Loving others. Working on building my relationship with God," she says. "I made a lot of decisions recently, one of which is to stop thinking in terms of when and then. '*When* I have this lined up, *then* I'll do this.' I can't spend my life always waiting for the right moment, or for the stars to align. I'd be waiting around forever. I also want to stop running from things and start running *to* them. I want to run to *you*," she says, smiling.

Johnny is floored. This is coming from the woman who's defined herself by her work for as long as he's ever known her. From the time they met in college when she was the star of the basketball team to these most recent years that she's been working for Diego. She's always equated her self-worth with her job, all the way back to when she was a college basketball player.

"You do?" he says softly.

"I do. Sure, working for Diego has been a lot of fun, but our conversation that day in his office really woke me up. I remembered my college coaching tell me one day about the Mack Truck Theory."

"I remember that!"

"Right? It's so good. The theory being that if you're the world's greatest heart surgeon and a Mack Truck hits and kills you one day, all the world's heart surgeries don't stop. The guy or girl who was second best then becomes the world's greatest, and life goes on. The world keeps spinning," she says.

"Very powerful," he says.

"I know. So while I've been working for Diego, I've been thinking that I'm the world's greatest heart surgeon."

"Not operating on me. No, ma'am," Johnny says.

"You know what I mean! Okay, so I thought I was the world's greatest executive manager of an automotive company. But I learned that day in speaking with him that it isn't about me. It never has been. Heck, *he* started the company, and it's not even about *him*."

"*Ph.D.*, right? Passion, humility, and discipline?" Johnny says.

"Exactly. *Ph.D.* And these last few months have had me rethinking my priorities. Starting with spending more time with friends and family," she says.

"Good for you! How was the beach, by the way?" he asks. "I never got around to asking you."

"It was phenomenal. Cameron's engaged!"

"Wow! That's awesome!"

"I know, it's insane. She waited until we got down there to tell me. Riley proposed to her when they were in New York for a work trip. Central Park. Sunset. The pictures are gorgeous. I'm so happy for them," Jenni says.

"That's great," Johnny says. "So with these newfound priorities of yours, what do they have you doing on a Saturday afternoon?' he asks. He gets up and walks into his kitchen.

"I thought you'd never ask," she says. "Come downstairs."

He stops in his tracks.

"What?"

"I said come downstairs! You can find out what I'm up to on this Saturday afternoon!"

He hangs up the phone and throws it on the couch, grabs his keys, and is out the door. He lives in a third-floor walk-up and races down the stairs, bursting through the door that leads outside.

As he does, he sees her.

Jenni's standing in front of his building looking as beautiful as she's ever been. He's seen her for mere seconds, but he can already see the changes in her. She's smiling from ear to ear. She looks fitter than she has in a long time, like she's been working out routinely. Her skin looks healthy. She's bouncing on her toes. She's practically glowing.

"Are you kidding me?!" he screams and runs toward her. She's laughing and crying and all of it put together.

She jumps into his arms, and he spins her around. As she nuzzles into his neck, she thinks, *I'm in a movie.*

He lets her down and leans back to really take her in.

"I can't believe it," he says.

"Believe it, babe," she says.

"I can't. How did you?"

"I knew you'd be home this weekend and wanted to do something to let you know how serious I am."

"How serious you are," he says.

"About us. How serious I am about us. I want to do it, Johnny. I want to take the leap. I want to make this work."

"You do?" he says, choking up.

"I do. I love you, Johnny," she says.

"I love you, Jenni," he says. He leans in, and they kiss. A kiss that's been waiting almost a decade to happen. It's everything they'd imagined it to be.

Our girl Jenni realized some very important things when she sat across from Alamiro on that date. She decided to stop running from things, from *people*, and start running *toward* what she wants. She has surprised Johnny – *her forever car* - by flying out to San Francisco and professing her love for him. She's also surprised him with the growth she's made and the priorities she's shifted around. A lot has changed in only a few short months.

When they stop for a breath, he grabs her suitcase and they start to walk up to his apartment.

"But what about your job?" he asks. "What about Diego?"

"Well, I'm only here for a few days for the time being. I'll go back and then sort everything out with him. He'll find someone else, I have no doubt. I have to shoot my shot," Jenni says.

Johnny laughs.

"You're right, he will. I really can't believe I'm hearing you say all this. So much has changed," he says as they make their way through the door of his apartment.

"I know!" Jenni says excitedly. "So much *has* changed. But it's all good."

"It is all good, you know that. I'm so happy you know that."

"Yep, and speaking of being happy. I've realized that a lot of things make me happy. I've come to realize that I have to be happy inside first. I've had to light that fire inside me first. And I'm choosing to do that. And then other people – you, my family, my friends – can enhance that fire. Can fuel the flame. So I had to come to some realizations over these past few weeks and recognize some things about myself so that I could get here. So that I could get here *with you*," Jenni says.

They're sitting on the couch now, and she reaches forward for his hand.

"Sounds to me like nothing much else matters right now," Johnny says, smiling. "Not *things*, anyway. But the *people* matter. And I'm a person, and you know how I feel about you," he says.

"I do. I certainly do."

"So what do you want to do?"

"You mean today?"

"No, in general. Are you moving out here?"

"Am I?"

"I certainly hope so!" He lunges forward to embrace her, and they kiss again.

"Wait!" he leans back and looks into her eyes.

"What is it?" she says.

"What about your car?!"

Back on the East Coast for one final packing session before she moves to California for good, Jenni returns from her most recent test drive.

She's returned the Ferrari to Passion who instinctively wants her to choose another car. Jenni, polite as ever, takes her up on the offer and has now finished test driving a Subaru Outback. Responsible, economical, trustworthy. It makes a lot of sense that her next car should be all of those things. Passion fully expects her to leave the lot with the car in her possession, this time for good.

Jenni parks, gets out of the vehicle, and walks over to Passion, who's been standing in the shade of a tree watching Jenni pull back into the lot.

"Well," Passion says, "are you all set?"

"I'm all set," Jenni says, dropping the keys back into Passion's hand. She's smiling from ear to ear.

"I'm confused," Passion says. "Why are you handing me the keys?"

"Because I won't be needing the car."

"Won't be needing the car?" Passion says. "But it's free! I'm giving it to you *for free*! Nothing in life is free!"

"I understand that. And I sincerely appreciate it. I really do. But I can't take it," Jenni says. She looks off into the distance.

"May I ask why?"

"Well, I was driving today. And driving, and driving. And sure, this one's fun to drive. And responsible. And ethical. And economical. But I'm not ready to make a decision on a car. I've made an altogether different decision instead."

"Oh yes?"

"Yes. I've decided that the car I choose isn't the important part."

"It's not?" Passion asks.

"No, it's not. You've given me some wonderful options, Passion. You really have. And the thought of not having to pay for a car is amazing. But this whole process and these past few years have taught me so much about myself. What's important to me. What isn't. What I want to do with my life."

"What you want to do with your life…" Passion repeats.

"Yes. And I've realized that it's not about the car itself. It's about who's riding with me in the car. Who's in the roundabout with me, helping me yield and accelerate and exit, and all that good stuff," Jenni says. "And I'm moving!"

"You are?!"

"I am! I'm moving to California for a fresh start. The East Coast has always been my home, but I'm ready to take some real risks and do some new things. I don't have anything set up at the moment, but I think I want my next job to be remote. I want to get a puppy and be at home to raise it. I really want to be able to be at home. And that means that I won't need a car, at least for now."

"Why not? You'll still have to get around. Everything in California is spread out!" Passion says.

"Well, I've got my e-bike. I'll get exercise every day, and that bike can take me everywhere I need. And if I need a car for something special, I can rent one."

"I see…" Passion says. "What about Johnny?" she asks, looking around. She's become used to seeing him by Jenni's side when she comes to the lot.

"He's taken a new job in California. That's why I'm moving out there. I've learned some things about myself these last few months, and I really want to be with him. I think I've known this on some level for a long time, but he's the one."

"You're dating?!"

"Yes! Sorry, it's so new that I haven't had much time to tell everyone. We've sort of been focusing on each other at the moment."

"That's okay. I'm happy for you," Passion says, smiling.

"Thank you so much. Yeah, he and I lost touch for a little bit. I wasn't myself. I got too caught up with my work, and I was focused on the wrong things. But now, I'll have more time to myself. And I'm excited to be with Johnny and see what all that holds."

"I see," Passion says smiling, putting the car keys into her pocket. "Did you say goodbye to Diego?"

"I did. It was really hard because I've honestly grown to love him, but my new life is waiting for me in California.

And I'm sorry to return the car, but this is the right decision. For me."

"I get it. But Jenni, you have to know that while I was forgiving of you and your mistakes, the real world *will not be forgiving*. The real world often gives you one shot to get something right. A car, a friendship, a career, a marriage. While I've shown you grace and mercy and forgiveness, you've got to learn from what happened with those cars you chose and how none of them ended up being right for you," Passion says.

"I know," Jenni says. "I took a lot of the wrong exits, Passion. And I've learned a lot. I *am learning* a lot."

"I feel that you are, yes," Passion says. "Take all of these experiences with you as you move forward and use them to guide you in the future. You've got Johnny to take care of now too. He's going to need that girl from college who made pretty much every shot she took. He's going to need the confident, self-assured Jenni. She's still in there. I saw it the first day I met you on the lot," Passion says.

"You did?" Jenni asks.

"I did. It's *courage*, my dear. That's what you have. The vast majority of people don't have it. You do. That's your secret power. And with it, I'm sure your best days are still ahead of you," Passion says, smiling.

"Thank you," Jenni says.

"So I guess I won't be seeing you around here anymore then?" Passion asks.

"I would say no, not for the time being. But who knows what the future holds?" Jenni says, starting to back away slowly, smiling.

"Absolutely!" Passion says, playfully punching a fist in the air. "Who knows what it holds?" she yells.

"Thank you again," Jenni says, and she turns to walk away.

"Wait, my dear," Passion says, holding up a hand.

Jenni turns back. "Yes?" she says.

"Take my business card. In case you ever need help, or a car, or a friend." Passion reaches out to hand Jenni a small white card with bright red lettering.

"Thank you so much, Passion. If I ever do need a car, you know I'll be calling you. But next time, I'll pay it forward. Give someone else the opportunity you've given me," she says. They both smile and come together for a warm hug. Jenni doesn't want to leave quite yet, and Passion can tell.

"Well, it sure is fun standing around shootin' the breeze, but you better get going, girl! The sun's setting, and you've got to walk home, I suspect."

"You're right! I do. Thank you, Passion!" Jenni says, excitedly turning to walk away.

And as Jenni starts down the path that leads to the road home, Passion intently watches her walk away. Passion helped Jenni in a variety of ways, she really did, but Jenni learned that she has to help herself. She has to find that happiness and contentment from *within*. And pursue the things she really wants in life. And that those things are not *things*.

They're people.

They're *Johnny*.

Passion smiles as Jenni turns the final corner of the car lot, stepping confidently toward the setting sun, disappearing from Passion's sight.

Jenni found success and *found herself along the way*, Passion thinks to herself. *Funny how that worked out.*

With a twinkle in her eye, Passion pats her own heart and shuts her eyes.

My own eyes fly open as I awake from my dream, the charter bus jolting me in my seat. I can hear the hydraulics exhale in a whoosh. We're pulling through the four-way stop as we pass my friend's car lot.

I blink several times to shed the sleep from my eyes.

We're still at that stop sign? I think to myself. *Wasn't that Jenni back there on the car lot? That wasn't "One-Shot."*

I look closely back into the distance, squinting. It takes a few seconds, but I spot the woman I'd thought was Jenni.

It's not her. Not even close.

Ah, well. Even so. I haven't seen her in forever, but I know I'll see her in a roundabout way sometime soon.

Today and Every Day, TWO FEET IN...

~ *Heather*

TWOFEETIN

About John Pennisi:

John Pennisi recently began his 17th year as a classroom English teacher. He has taught both middle school and high school at private schools in Maryland and Virginia. Currently, he serves as a Middle School English Teacher and the Upper School Dean of Students at Wakefield School in The Plains, Virginia.

John holds both a B.S. in Biology from Lenoir-Rhyne College in Hickory, North Carolina, and an M.A. in English Literature and Composition from Washington College in Chestertown, Maryland. He is currently working toward completing a professional sequence in technical communication from the University of California, Berkeley.

In addition to teaching, John has also coached boys and girls basketball for many years, including an assistant coaching position with the varsity boys basketball program at St. Mary's Ryken High School in Leonardtown, Maryland (a Washington Catholic Athletic Conference school). He has been an English Department Chair. He has earned teaching awards from the Archdiocese of Washington; Johns Hopkins; University of Maryland, Baltimore County; and Stanford University. He has founded chapters of the Interact Club (a Rotary Club-sponsored community service organization) at both his current and previous schools.

John has published poetry in both the *Santa Clara Review* and Politics & Prose's anthology *District Lines*. He enjoys watching college basketball, reading, writing, and spending time with his nephews. He lives in northern Virginia.

About Heather Macy:

Heather Macy is a leading elite performance coach and one of only 300 EQ-certified basketball coaches in the country. In addition to one-on-one coaching and consulting, she currently travels around the country educating teams, coaches, and organizations on how to use EQ to become an elite performer. Several of these presentations are currently published on CoachTube.com for download. She has been a speaker at some of the top coaching clinics and professional development events in the country, including USA Basketball and Nike Championship Clinics. Coach Macy is also a frequent speaker at corporate and leadership events on the topics of leadership, teamwork, accountability, and discipline. She is currently hosting a 1-hour weekly Rising Coaches TV series discussing her book, *Two Feet Forward: Everyday Lessons in Leadership.* This book was a #1 new release in basketball coaching on Amazon.

Combined with her EQ Certification, in the spring of 2020, Coach Macy also received a specialization in Positive Psychology from the University of Pennsylvania.

With regard to basketball, Coach Macy is entering her third season with the Pride after being named head coach and Assistant Director of Athletics on September 24, 2020. Last year, Coach Macy led the Pride to a share of the regular season USA South East Division Championship, with a 17-1 conference record and 25-2 overall, the best in school history. The Pride won 18 consecutive games until falling in the semi-finals of the conference tournament. She mentored two players to the All USA South First team, and her team finished in the top 10 of scoring offenses nationally, at over 84 points per game, as well as 9th nationally in scoring margin (24.4 points) and 13th nationally in field goal percentage (34.2%). She earned her 300th career victory in Greensboro's February 12th win over Meredith.

In her first season as Pride Head Coach, the team started the season 1-7. GC ultimately finished the year with a 6-9 record, placing fourth in the conference.

Macy came back to the Pride family with more than 20 years of college coaching experience, including 15 years as a head coach. Most recently, Macy served as the head women's basketball coach at Spartanburg Methodist College. During her lone season with the Pioneers, Macy led her team to Region X regular-season and tournament championships while posting a 21-8 record and being named Region X Coach of the Year.

Prior to her one-year stint with the Pioneers, Macy served as the head women's basketball coach at NCAA Division I, East Carolina University. Macy made her mark on the Pirates' record books during her eight-year tenure as she became the all-time winningest coach in ECU history with 134 victories. Macy also led the purple and gold to three straight 20-win seasons (2013-2015) and earned Conference USA Coach of the Year honors in 2013 after her team posted an overall record of 22-10, while going 11-5 in conference play.

Before making the jump to the Pirates, Macy served as a head coach on the NCAA Division II level for five seasons. She coached three seasons at Francis Marion University (2007-2010) and two seasons at Pfeiffer University (2005-2007). While at Francis Marion, Macy became the first women's basketball coach in the Peach Belt Conference's history to win back-to-back Coach of the Year honors and guided her squads to three straight appearances in the NCAA Division II tournament, including a trip to the Sweet 16 in 2009. In addition to her honors at Francis Marion, Macy also earned CVAC (now known as Conference Carolinas) Coach of the Year accolades in 2007 after leading Pfeiffer to a 26-5 record.

In addition to her time as a head coach, Macy also spent time as an assistant coach on the Division I (High Point and UMBC) and Division II levels, which started at Catawba College immediately following her graduation from Greensboro College.

While obtaining her B.S. in Sport and Exercise Studies (Cum Laude) from Greensboro, Macy was a four-year member of the Pride women's basketball team. During her playing career, Macy placed her name in the Greensboro College record books for three-point field goals attempted and made, while also ranking 9th in all-time games played with 105. She was also inducted into the Greensboro College Athletics Hall of Fame as a member of the 1996 women's basketball team on March 31, 2012. In addition to the Greensboro College Hall of Fame, Macy was also inducted into the Starmount High School Hall of Fame.

In addition to her degree from Greensboro College, Macy also holds an M.S. in Human Performance and Recreation with a concentration in Administration from the University of Southern Mississippi.

For more information on Coach Heather Macy, please visit her website at Go2FeetIn.com or follow her on social media @2FeetInCoaching.

Made in the USA
Columbia, SC
28 August 2024